Corporate America: They Had A Plot But God Had A Plan

The Employee's Handbook:
Tools and Techniques for navigating through the practical and emotional challenges of gender, race, sexual orientation, age, religious discrimination, and sexual harassment

by

Betty Marie Knight

authorHOUSE

1663 LIBERTY DRIVE, SUITE 200
BLOOMINGTON, INDIANA 47403
(800) 839-8640
www.authorhouse.com

© *2004 Betty Marie Knight*
All Rights Reserved.

No part of this book may be reproduced, stored in a retrieval system, or transmitted by any means without the written permission of the author.

First published by AuthorHouse 08/26/04

ISBN: 1-4184-1739-4 (e)
ISBN: 1-4184-1740-8 (sc)

Printed in the United States of America
Bloomington, Indiana

This book is printed on acid-free paper.

TELL ME WHEN AND WHERE DID THEY CROSS THE LINE?

The Employee's Handbook

Self Help

Be on the lookout for Betty's Bits

Tragedy or Strategy – it is all in the way you perceive it.

A Tragedy is accepting extreme exposures and not equipping and/or enlightening others with what has been learned from these experiences - not enforcing the expertise learned.

A Strategy is using every tragedy to expedite experiences, and exercising your influences, exercising your expertise by executing what you have learned exceedingly and abundantly above every expectation.

From Segregation
To Integration
To Discrimination
To Education
Equals Reformation and Restoration!

Reformation means to correct, amend, to make right. Restoration means to place one back to its original state. "In His image and after His Likeness."

Be On the Look out for Betty's Bits

Betty's Bits are powerful nuggets of wisdom you will see throughout the book!

Education the root word is Educate

Embracing

Diversities

Unifying

Corporate

America

Towards

Investing Into

One

Nation

The Constitution of the United States says "One Nation under God indivisible with liberty and justice for all!

Leathers, Feathers, and Furs

Water Walkers come to mind when you see these three people.
We have the Faith that can conquer anything. Thanks to Stevie.

Special thanks

Special thanks to one of my best friends, Wanda Clemmons: *Wanda Clemmons is one of the most gifted persons you would ever want to meet. Wanda walked with me five years through all of this. She cried with me, she laughed with me, she encouraged me, she pushed me, she advised me. As a matter of fact, Wanda is the one that said to me* **"They had a Plot But God had a Plan."** *After she said it I thought to myself, "I'm going to use that statement for a poem or something." Well, around August 20th 2001, I woke up and began to take my journal off the shelf and write chapters for my case at the EEOC. At the beginning of each new idea or thought I had about Corporate America, I was wrapped up in so much pain. I wrote this chapter titled "Termination vs. Determination" and I realized that I was writing a book. Then* the full name came to me for a title. **"Corporate America, They Had A <u>Plot</u> But God Had A <u>Plan</u>."**

Wanda Clemmons is the founder of the Los Angeles Destiny Center. L.A. Times wrote an article about her, called "A lesson in Determination." However, that does not fully define this water walker, Wanda Clemmons. She should have gone to school to be a lawyer because she has a remarkable knowledge of law. After the Holy Spirit revealed to me what to write, she would confirm almost every word with her insight into legal matters. Wanda is an educator and she has a grasp on destiny like no one else I have ever met, I want to thank her for being there for me through thick and thin. Wanda Clemmons' friendship is one that I pray every human being will have the chance to experience in this lifetime. **Wanda, thank you for being a friend.**

Mother Doss, I thank God for this lady right here; she encouraged me in so many ways. She is my Naomi, The Lone Ranger had his Ton toe, Lucy had her Ricky, Batman had his Robin and well, Betty Knight has her Doris Doss. Thank you, mother, for your push to finish this book, and your spiritual

insight that helped me continue when I wanted to quit—and she knows what I mean.

Maxine Crawford, a dear friend of mine for over 15 years. We started the prayer line in September 1990 on the floor of 14028 South Budlong Ave., in Gardena, California. We lay prostrate in the center of my front room floor and we requested four specific things from God. In 2001 we started a prayer line again; we had gone through the same challenges and together we overcame everything the devil threw at us. We had stored up the prayers back in September of 1990 concerning four specific things. Little did we know that we would come out together in November 2001, that the things we had made known unto God, and having done all to stand, we would be found standing still in June 2002, looking unto Jesus the Author and Finisher of our Faith. Thanks, Maxine, together we made it. I can't think of anyone better to have come through this with. Remember, in due season we will reap because we did not faint. Whatever you do DON'T FAINT!

Thirdly, Brother Arturo and Patricia Spates, thank you for all of your spiritual insight of warfare. God's infinite wisdom allowed you to train me over 20 years ago concerning warfare so that I would survive the <u>Battles of my Life</u>! I learned that the Battles were not mine they were the Lords'. Thank you both.

Last, but certainly not least, Tanishia, Jasmine, Dominigue for being in my life because I had testified about God's deliverance so much I had to hold on for them to see that this God I had bragged on was every bit as great as I said He was and that He was able to do exceedingly, abundantly above all I dare to ask, think or desire. He did just what He said He would.

To my son, Denair McBride, thank you for being the most wonderful person that God could place in a man, and Nicole is a special woman to have you as a husband and Jayln is just as special to have you as a dad. I am very proud of you.

To everyone that reached out to me in my time of need, with just a smile, a kind word that gave me the strength to keep going, Sharon, Linda, Barbara, Shelly, Vera Lewis, and to my brothers and sisters in Christ. Many thanks to my Pastor, Bishop Noel Jones, who spoke so many words to every gift in me and who would not allow me to bury any of them. To all my friends, *thank you for whatever you did to help me be the best I could be. Thanks to all of you.*

Special thanks to Anthony for the photo on the back cover.

Betty's Bits

Betty's Bits*:* While sitting in front of my Compaq around 10:55 A.M. Saturday morning I was overwhelmed with this e-mail. This was an S.O.S. to African-Americans everywhere titled "Our Right To Vote." I quote, "Below you will find a speech that a popular star's wife gave at a function. This is extremely important. We are quickly approaching the 21st Century and we were wondering, and when I say we, I mean others of us out there who wonder if everyone else out there knows what the significance of the year 2007 is to black America? Did you know that our right to VOTE would expire in the year of 2007? Seriously! The Voters Right Act signed in 1965 by Lyndon B. Johnson was just an ACT. It was not a law. In 1982, Ronald Reagan amended the Voters Right ACT for another 25 years. Which means that in the year 2007 we could lose the Right to Vote! Does anyone realize that African-Americans are the only group of people who require PERMISSION under the United States Constitution to Vote! In the year 2007, Congress will once again convene to decide whether or not blacks should retain the rights to vote (crazy but true). Our right to vote should have never been up for discussion, review and/or evaluation." "I did my research and found out that the fourteenth and fifteen Amendments set our voting rights in tack. The EEOC was birthed out of Civil Rights Act. The EEOC is like the watchdog created by the government to make sure there are fair employment, fair treatment, and fair housing for the African-American/minorities, and anyone who is being discriminated against. However, to all African-American's who are not exercising their right to vote with the cope out "My vote won't count," just think if this e-mail was true, your vote wouldn't count!" "One Vote! One Voice!"

APPEAL, I'm APPALLED!

Corporate America "They Had A Plot But God Had A Plan" Part II

Could "Binding Arbitration" be the culprit behind Corporate? "Binding Arbitration" gives a company the thin line to cross to violate your civil rights. Arbitration keeps them out of the courtroom, from a judge and from a jury. This statement is not for/or against all companies, only to the companies that intend to practice discrimination.

I am appalled that discrimination still has this great stronghold in America today. I am appalled that I received the same injustice from an investigator in the Los Angeles EEOC office. I called the EEOC office in Washington D.C. and spoke with the department head concerning the discrimination within the EEOC. I had witnesses, evidence, and testimonies that my Civil Rights were being violated. To add insult to injury, my credible expert witness who took a stand on my behalf, when everyone else was hiding and changing their testimony was given a verbal warning, a written warning and then fired in the same day after speaking with the company's attorney in her deposition affirming that my Civil Rights were violated. She stated in her own words that she had documents plus made the CEO aware on several occasions that I was being discriminated against. I am appalled!

The racial current is so at the forefront as it was revealed when that employee went "postal" in Dallas, Texas in the 90s. Those in authority are using their power to influence and/or destroy peoples' lives, livelihood, credit, and families—especially after an employee's loyalty and productivity has aided the company's success. These employees come to work in sickness or in health, for better or worse, and are not planning on retiring until 65 or until death do them apart. I am appalled. I believe that Binding Arbitration is the culprit behind corporate. Binding Arbitration will set a limited course of the monetary amount awarded for the damages and determines the account and penalty the company will receive if found guilty violating an employee's Civil Rights. This makes violations easy—I am appalled!

Prologue

This book is not for the faint at heart. Nor is it an indictment of all corporations. It is an evaluation of many corporations in America. But until we truly critically analyze where we are today, we cannot reach that pinnacle where we are truly one nation under God with liberty and justice for all. Nor will we totally be unified and identified in Corporate America. Until we speak out of our own mouths against discrimination, then and only then can we hear it and face what we have swept under the rugs of pretense when discrimination is obviously staring us all in the face. The new name is "Modern Day Lynching."

Corporate America, you should be careful, very careful, if you are allowing those in upper management who are biased, prejudiced or do not believe that all men and women are created equal, to discriminate against others. Don't assume that employees that are discriminated against or harassed will quit. Some of us are fighters. Don't assume that an employee is an average employee that will go along with the violations. Corporate America, you don't know who your employees know. You don't know who your employees' are/or who they're related to. My Big Brother is a Jew. Don't assume they don't know their Civil Rights. Don't assume that we can't prove harassment/discrimination. That's my reason for writing this book. I know my case is not an isolated case, and I know someone needs my help in "How to Survive in a Hostile and Offensive Work Environment." If I sound a little angry I am; there is a righteous indignation within me after what I experienced in Corporate America here in the 21st Century. Not because of what they did but because they really believed they could do it and get away with it. If my cross can be someone's crown, then all my pain was not in vain, and if this book enlightens others I will know that all things worked together for the good of those that love the Lord and are called according to His purpose. My friend wrote my resignation letter, because she was a witness to so much of the discrimination I received in this workplace. One manager resigned because of *what she saw me endure, and felt if she remained at this company she would be forced to compromise her own integrity.*

One of my friend's, friend worked at a company in Ontario and Sharon was in charge of the woman in Human Resource. The Human Resource manager was made aware of my situation by my new co-worker and she was very unhappy with the way the managers were hurting me. Linda saw with her own eyes that I was not doing anything to deserve the harassment and discrimination, and she perceived that this in no way was going to stop. After she told her friend in Ontario, California about what this job's management was doing to me, Sharon took up my cause. This same lady went to a lawyer and the human resource manager helped her put the charges in writing. They confirmed that this was surely discrimination. They helped me get my charge ready for the EEOC. What I'm saying is this, "You Never Know Who We Know." W. Ross Winterowd and Geoffrey R. Winterowd wrote, "The Critical Reader, Thinker, and Writer" and stated, **"***If you want to join the ongoing battle against rights abuse, the first thing to do is to learn as much as you can about them. Already published materials are not enough. A sudden change in government, or a single law, can bring about enormous* *changes in human rights almost overnight." Corporate America, it is dangerous to push someone into a corner; that person then realizes that they have "Nothing to Lose." A lawsuit is in view. Corporate America acts as though it wears a bulletproof vest, but I'm the arrow in the hand of the Father; I will penetrate through the deception of discrimination. I am a "Secret Weapon." Yes, it will be rough for a while, yes, you will be isolated for a while, and yes, you may be blackballed for a while. Yes, you will have to believe God and look for other means of support for a while. But if you follow my advice you will talk to others about your situation—lawyers, loved ones and support groups, because in the multitude of counsel there is safety. To every one that hath an ear to hear let him hear: This is a warning to the foolish and advice to the wise. I speak these words by the Spirit; take heed that you do unto others, as you would have them do unto you. After this book hits the stands, discrimination will no longer be invisible. Through me, God has provided a face that is expressive, a mouth that can speak out, a voice that can articulate, a nose that can smell.* **It has a stint in God's nostril,** *ears that can hear, eyes that can recognize, arms that will no longer embrace discrimination. I speak with a deep conviction that in 2003-2004* *the largest cases in the history of America will be fought and won against discrimination. I challenge you to change or be held accountable.*

In my case, I would have had a very serious complex if people around me had not confirmed to me that my Civil Rights were being violated? Discrimination is not exclusive to race; discrimination comes in many shapes and sizes. Homosexuals are not discriminated against because of their gender, but because of their alternate lifestyle. God hates the sin but He loves the sinner. Discrimination leaves you feeling irrelevant, incompetent, and isolated. You must trust God and move forward. Last and certainly not least, a person being discriminated against could be a child of God that God has equipped and sent to reap a harvest that no one would take a stand against. God has taken this vessel through continued trials and strengthened me to go into Corporate America and expose every trick of the devil for His glory. I was one of those vessels that was sent into Corporate America to let my light so shine before men that they may see my good works but give glory to the Father in Heaven. This was For His Glory!

Rosa Parks is one of the women that I cherish for the stand she took, which gave birth to the Montgomery Boycott Movement. Rosa Parks revealed to me, in her convictions, that by refusing to give up her seat while simultaneously taking a stand in her heart that there are some barriers which only a black woman can break—some things in life God intends for women only." It's not optional; it is essential, that a woman be involved. I believe if a black man had taken this same stand he would have been beaten or killed. However, they had to respect Rosa Parks' gender, even when they could not respect her genealogy.

Harriett Tubman is another woman that has helped shape my life and set my heart to endure discrimination for my convictions. She took a stand and set the slaves free, which gave birth to the Underground Railroad. I believe I have the calling of these great women; I have been anointed to set the captive free.

Betty's Bits: The purpose for bearing and sharing my experiences was never to win a lawsuit nor is it for legal advice. However, these tools and techniques are for Corporate America to become sensitive of all the many diversities that must be embraced to work harmoniously. When and if these tools are embraced we won't loose our cultural flavor, distinction, individuality <u>or</u> our balance, we will just blend together and become one nation under God, indivisibly, with liberty and justice for all.

Introduction

This book truly has the flavor of Esther; in the book of Esther, God Almighty is hardly mentioned and there were times He was not seen. However, there is evidence that God was surely there. The only spiritual sign is when Esther asks the maiden to fast with her before she goes to see the king.

During my life in Corporate America there were times when I could not see God. I'm not stiff in my convictions nor am I religious; however, there is evidence that God was in control of everyone involved. Employees from different departments testified to help me, even some employees who had left the company but were witnesses to what I had gone through testified on my behalf. Linda and Sharon took up my cause, and shared with a Human Resource manager what was being done to me. God was there when I saw a lawyer, he gave me legal advice without having me sign a retainer. God was there when I went through surgery and He released me from this job so I could heal physically. God touched the hearts of everyone that crossed my path and moved them to assist me in the writing of this book. It was God's timing when I was delivered from Corporate America's plot not only to fire me but also to humiliate me. It was God whom I saw when I survived numerous breast cysts and not one was cancerous. God was there when I survived the negative remarks and slurs, yet, still I believed that I am more than a Conqueror.

    Yes, I know God was there!

Be on the lookout for Betty's Bits

Dedication

I would like to dedicate this book to a special man, J.E. Craig, who I've known and learned to respect in a great way, and in a short period of time. He is a man of great integrity with very strong convictions to pursue his dreams and fulfill his purpose in such a way that's inspiring me to have the courage to fulfill all of my dreams. James put the E in ennoble and the E in enable. A man that walks in all of his God given authority, and is very courageous in all that he puts his hands to do, and whatever he does, he leaves no stone unturned.

I realized in a greater way through James that my steps have purpose!

Discrimination vs. Terrorist Attack

This book reminds me of the New York terrorist attack in America, on September 11, 2001. My civil rights faced a 911 terrorist attack that lasted over seven years in Corporate America. My self-esteem, ethnicity, character, integrity—the very essence of my soul—took a blow below the belt that still has me reeling. I received an e-mail that helps me to identify and realize that my character was constantly being assassinated and I was viewed negatively in the workplace because of my race.

This hostile work environment caused me to take a very bold stand; I was determined not to lose my focus of destiny. My life's mission statement herald out of my innermost being, ***"My present position is not an indication of my future potential."*** It also resounded from a wall plaque of my work area.

Through this extremely difficult and challenging experience I birthed *Corporate America They Had A Plot, But God Had A Plan.* This book takes a riveting look at Corporate America's discrimination through the eyes of an employee who only wanted to build-up not tear down, help not hinder, add not take away. The reason why this attack felt like a terrorist attack is because my stand was against the root of all evil – MONEY! The stand I took was coming up against the three largest moneymaking businesses: the lawyers' personnel, the company's personnel and the insurance company's personnel. This became the stand of all stands and this person of color would set a precedent.

White America has not felt the brunt of humiliation, degradation, or isolation of discrimination as black America has. Just as the counterfeiters learn how to update their currency to deceive merchants, Corporate America has learned to update discrimination and deceive minorities into believing that it is no longer discrimination but unfairness. My faith and courage to stand is what made me more than a conqueror.

Black women have always opposed the odds

I've read several books about black women opposing the odds. When I read *Within the Plantation Household: Black and White Women of the Old South* I wanted to quote this section from Elizabeth Fox-Genovese's point of view.

After what I experienced in Corporate America I thought about my ancestors of strong black women and how they survived. They were human beings that were born in a society, which disapproved of their very existence. What is it that we possess, what is it that is recognized as a threat even by our own culture? Something within us communicates through our innermost being that we possess a power greater than what we even know or understand. I tried to get an understanding from studying the book *Within the Plantation Household: Black and White Women of the Old South: Women who Opposed Slavery.* I looked up the word slave - a captive, a person without freedom or personal rights. Work like a slave. In my study I would like for you to see a repeat of the 1800's slavery, through the eyes of Corporate America. Take a look through my eyes and tell me do you see what I see? A Servant or A Slave? Look carefully there is a difference.

Slaveholders' sexual exploitation of slave women further shredded the illusions of a harmonious white and black family. Resistance wasn't possible, especially if the master was the perpetrator. "Plenty of the colored women have children by the white man. She knew better than to not do what he say." Young masters presented a more complicated problem. Whites knew as well as blacks that the young men were likely to claim sexual prerogatives with the slave women, and frequently sought to remove the young women from temptation by sending them away to school.

The Supreme Court conceded the difficulty with respect to punishment: "Absolute obedience, and subordination to the lawful authority of the master, are the duty of the slave.... The law cannot enter into strict scrutiny of the precise force employed by the master, with view of ascertaining that the chastisement had or had not been reasonable." The law did hold masters accountable for what it defined as wanton murder, but not for accidental deaths, and assuredly not for sexual assault. I believe these things were done to these women because they were black; the thought of a white woman being treated like this is unheard of. Well, keep reading, because here we are in 2000 and these people in Corporate America treated white women like they treated me. The company turned its attention to discrediting Linda as my witness in my case. Linda liked me as a human being, took a stand, and she was treated the same way I was. I discerned their next move so Linda and I went to the EEOC office. However, since I knew their strategy, I was able to help her beat them at their own game.

Accountability - means to be made liable to be held responsible; able to be explained.

Discrimination - 1) the ability to see small differences or make careful and good choices. 2.) The treating of some people better than others for an unfair reason.

Betty's Bits: What is it about this Black woman? It is her strength? It is, "A strength that's not her own." Many women posses it and it is seen in every angle, it depends on how much the black woman is willing and comfortable with being and revealing who she really is. Oprah Winfrey, posses this kind strength and it is expressed in her giving. Halle Berry posses this kind of strength and it is expressed in her acting ability. Betty Knight posses this strength and it is expressed in her vocal and writing skills. Keep looking because who ever possess this kind of strength it cannot be hidden, you are "A Private Vision Aiming for Public View."

Table of Contents

Special thanks xi

Betty's Bits... xvii

APPEAL, I'm APPALLED! xix

Prologue xxiii

Introduction xxix

Dedication xxxi

Discrimination vs. Terrorist Attack xxxiii

Black women have always opposed the odds xxxv

"Differences" by Linda Chapman xliii

Chapter 1
HOW TO SURVIVE IN A HOSTILE WORK ENVIRONMENT 1

Chapter 2
I SURVIVED 8

Chapter 3
SIGNS THAT ALERT YOU TO RECOGNIZE UNFAIRNESS OR DISCRIMINATION 20

Chapter 4
THEY HAD A PLOT BUT GOD HAD A PLAN 25

Are You Experiencing Trouble in Corporate America? 29

Chapter 5
TEAM PLAYERS 32

Crossing the Line 39

Chapter 6
CULTURAL DIVERSITIES 41

Cultural DiversitiesBeing black in the Workplace 44

Rules 46

From Segregation to Integration 47

Chapter 7
THE SECRECT CORPORATE AMERICA DOES NOT WANT YOU TO KNOW! 49

Chapter 8
SETUPS 52

Gathering Evidence 62

Nine-One-One 64

Chapter 9
CRUCIFIED CROSS EXPERIENCE 68

Chapter 10
KAISER PSYCHIATRIC CARE 75

Work Stress Program 76

THE PRIVATE INVESTIGATOR INVESTIGATES THE COUNSELOR 86

Chapter 11
CIVIL VS. FEDERAL 91

Chapter 12
WHAT IFS 95

Chapter 13
NAVIGATING UP THE CORPORATE LADDER 101

Chapter 14
DISCERNING THE ATMOSPHERE..104
Discerning Atmospheres Solutions for/In 107

Chapter 15
A PLOT VS. A PLAN 109
ALL MEN 114

Chapter 16
WHAT QUALIFIES ME 116

Chapter 17
CORPORATE CONSPIRACY 120
Beyond Faith—Trust...125
The 23rd Psalms for the Workplace 128

Chapter 18
TERMINATION VS. DISCRIMINATION 131

Chapter 19
STRESS OR TEST 136

Chapter 20
GO THROUGH MEDIATION 141

Chapter 21
SABOTAGE CHARACTER 151
Who Sets The Tone? 151

Chapter 22
TRANSITION FROM HOME BACK TO WORK 156

Chapter 23
A LESSON FROM A FROG 167
Appendix A 172
Appendix B 174
Facts Sheets on Discrimination..174
BIBLIOGRAPHY 183

"Differences" by Linda Chapman

From an Italian woman's point of view:

"Women have many characteristics in common and yet when all is said and done I have witnessed, on more than one occasion, a basic difference that takes me back each time. I am speaking of a cultural imbalance that exists between African-American women and the rest of us. ***This phenomenon does not exist between any other races of women.***

Betty and I became friends almost immediately in 1998 when I began working for the same company. Betty and I were part of the 2000 Walk/Run for Breast Cancer in Los Angeles. We began walking around the massive grounds where all the booths had been constructed and where women of all ages and races gathered to pick up some of the "goodies" that were given out to participants. This is where it all began and the differences between us became apparent. Each time a black woman would walk toward us, she and Betty would nod, smile and say, "Hey there, how are you doing?" I turned and questioned, "Betty, do you know that woman?" "No" came the answer. In my mind, I could hear myself saying something similar to "Wow!" My awareness led me to witness this interaction time and again.

Black women would nod at one another in passing on the street, in stores and, needless to say, in the workplace. I thought I was warm with just about everyone at the company. Others and I would smile and greet one another in passing and it felt great. Nevertheless, one day, Betty and I were walking to another building and Gloria, a very beautiful, sweet and affectionate woman who worked in another department was walking toward us. It was, for a fleeting moment, as if I was not even there. It would take too many words and pictures to explain the greeting I witnessed between these two women. The smiles that looked almost like laughter, the hugs that embraced all they stood for, and the words that said so much more than "Hey there." Jealously reared and my response to both of them was, "Hey how come ya'll don't greet me like that?" They both looked at me as if they did not understand my question. You see, these women do not even know they have a unique quality between them that no other women possess. What is natural to them is supernatural to me, what is ordinary to them is extraordinary to me, what's so normal to them is abnormal to me, and yet this race possesses it. I challenge all women to open their eyes and embrace this part of black culture that is seriously lacking in the rest of us. Women would become much closer as a sex and much more in tune with one another's feeling.

Oh, by the way did I mention that Betty is a beautiful, loving black woman?"

Chapter 1

HOW TO SURVIVE IN A HOSTILE WORK ENVIRONMENT

When I began to work in this field as a Inventory Controller everything was great. I was excited about learning filing, inventory, flags, accounting, and posting. I had been a housewife for over 15 years and these were new challenges, a new horizon. I wanted to find my place in Corporate America and do my part for society.

When you first begin a job a personal file is started on you. This file is their diary about you. It is full of information good and bad. All your records are kept in your file, such as pay raises, evaluations, written warnings, etc. (You, in turn, should keep a diary or a journal on them, because fair exchange is no robbery).

Betty Marie Knight

The company has what is called an Employee Handbook. In the Table of Contents there are chapters, numbers and titles: (*Important, this Employee Handbook is not to protect you: I don't care if Chapter 1 says Equal Employment. This personnel file is used to help them keep good records on you. Be smart and keep records on them, you don't know what the future holds, and you don't want Corporate America to hold your future).

This Employee Handbook is to protect the company from you: Look very closely at the way it is written. Remember, all survivors will make the companies in Corporate America rewrite a portion of the Company's Employee Handbook because the survivor will bring to light something that the company and their lawyers have not witnessed before. Another chapter is then added in the Employee Handbook to protect them from you. In case of lawsuits, Corporate America will mention things in their diary about you that have passed the statute of limitations in order to build a case. But remember, "No weapon formed against you shall prosper." And every tongue that rises up against you shall be judged. The Scripture says, "They that have Godly Wisdom shall be sought after."

Corporate America: They Had A Plot But God Had A Plan

The wisdom of God was manifested to me at a very early stage of my employment in this company. There were employees that worked various duties in this company, which allowed them to be used when needed. For example, one employee's job responsibilities varied between clerk and switchboard operator. Switchboard operators had to punch in at 7:30 A.M. Monday through Friday. The switchboard had at least 22 lines and he handled them all "successfully." He was very knowledgeable of this company's procedures so when he decided to pull a robbery, it was easy for him and his accomplice. They knew what time to hit. They knew which way to hit. Time was set at early morning. This plot was well thought out by two people on the inside and they got away with it. Being switchboard operators, they knew when to call the men to pull the job.

I was told after management accomplished this plot, that managers had discussed the possibility of things like this happening. The people who worked within this company were stealing cars and getting away with it because preventive procedures were not being followed. They had cameras in the office but they were not connected. Several people on the inside knew about the cameras but some of us never knew that the cameras could not record and monitor the room. Well, after these people had robbed this company twice and gotten away with it twice, the company finally felt that there needed to be some changes made. They called for an investigator because between the two robberies over $15,000 to $25,000 had been stolen: The investigator comes in on a Monday, and gets a list from the business managers of every person that worked in the office. The atmosphere is now charged with negative energy, and everyone is very paranoid and offended.

The investigator interviewed all of us, and the question everyone was asked at the end of the interview was "Who do you think did it?" When this investigator interviewed me, this man was so fascinated with my insight, that he spent two weeks trying to understand the Holy Spirit and how He functions in me. I explained to him up front, that what I was about to say I could not prove, but there is a witness in me, a knowing in me that is going to reveal to you what was done, how it was done, where it was done.

After our last visit, he said, "When this investigation is over, I will have to give a report, one on one to the owner of this company. I am going to tell him about you; believe you me, you have played a vital part in this investigation." We went to breakfast and he thanked me for all my help. Well, the business manager told me, after this investigation was over that the owner had been made aware of this little African-American lady in his business office? However, they failed to see me as a valuable player on their team.

I survived working with twenty-five white women, three black women, and one man. I endured and survived strong hostility 8 hours a day, 40 hours or more per week. My friends said that the reason why I was attacked so violently was that I was:

- *Anointed*
- *African American*
- *Attractive*
- *A Female*
- **Intelligent and walked in wisdom because I am filled with the Holy Ghost.**

I had the Ancient of Days living in me and governing my life. I survived racial slurs, malice and plans to destroy me professionally and personally. I survived eight co-workers getting together, and going to the general manager to get me fired for not doing my job. I survived co-workers isolating, insulting, and ignoring me for several years. Isolation is a great tool Corporate America uses because isolation gives you a victim mentality. Isolation builds insecurities; I became insecure as a wife, as a mother, as a friend, as a speaker, as a motivator, which made me constantly question my own faith in God.

I survived by using my gifts always with a two-fold purpose. Say to yourself, "two-fold purpose!" I have a gift for writing poetry: God caused my gifts to flourish, so much so that I recognized that this talent was maturing and functioning at another level in this particular season of my life. So I knew somewhere around me was good soil and I had to be patient to find it. I planted this seed of love and watched love produce meekness, gentleness, temperance, faith, joy, peace, and longsuffering, and I reaped my Harvest.

Betty's Bits: Even though I walk in the flesh, I do not war after the flesh; for the weapon of my warfare is not carnal but mighty through God to the pulling down the enemy's stronghold. This warfare is a force of very negative energy, mostly in the mind. Corporate America can make you respond to what they are making you think, feel, see, without them ever carrying out their plot against you. They will use you to execute your own demise. The act of discrimination is 85% psychological (mind games) and 15% procedure. However, the intense study and skill gained by hand on hand combat enlightened me to help you successfully make Corporate America uncover what's undercover.

Corporate America: They Had A Plot But God Had A Plan

When you join the work force in Corporate America you will receive what is called and Employee's Handbook. This employee handbook is designed to do one of two things. The first thing it is designed to do is to inform you as to "What you can expect from that company," and the second thing it is designed to do is to inform you as to "What the company expect from you." Two-way communication. Pay close attention to clauses such as this.

__Betty's Bits:__ The content of this handbook, however, constitute only a summary of the employee benefits, personnel policies, and employment regulations in effect at the time of publication. This handbook should not be constructed as creating any kind of "employment contract," since the compnay has the ability to add, change or delete wages, benefits, policies and all other working conditions as it deems appropriate without obtaining another person's consent or agreement.

Chapter 2

I SURVIVED

I survived because I listened to, or perceived their thoughts through their greetings. You can locate a person by or through a greeting morning, noon, and night. Now there are some people who are not morning people. Only time can reveal who those people are; however, if they responded in their morning greeting to everyone in the same way they responded to you, then he or she could not be a morning person. But if their greeting is an offensive or a hostile tone, this individual has a challenge with you. So be very careful, especially if it is someone in authority. Don't become over-friendly just ask for wisdom and give it time. On the other hand, if this is a toxic person or a difficult person, keeping your distance is the best way to survive. Remember, if it's a snake it will bite you.

I survived because I had an ear to hear. I leaned to listen attentively, especially when I noticed that I was considered a disgruntled employee. I had begun to speak up on the many things I had used to ignore. As long as I took the derogatory remarks and stayed the brunt of the jokes, gave advice, helped solve problems, and did my work, I was an ideal employee. I discerned negative body language whenever certain managers talked to me and they always made certain comments that did not fit the subject we were discussing. Having an ear to hear, a signal would go off in me, "What did that have to do with what we were discussing?"

There is always a mouthpiece in Corporate America that is used to say or do their dirty work. This employee has a little authority—just enough to get themselves and the company into trouble. He/She will either have boldness or just be what is called a "bigmouth," and this employee with delegated authority can't hold water (meaning they could not keep anything confidential), repeating what is confidential made them feel in control. "But loose lips sink ships." This employee at my company would always alert me that the harassment was going to start. Not only by what she said but by what she didn't say.

Discern the atmosphere daily. I became so sensitive that I could discern if the day would be good or challenging before I even left home. (Refer to Chapter 14: A Spiritual Atmosphere to get a clearer understanding of this.)

I Survived

My friend would always say to me, "Betty, the reason you are so violently attacked is because you are anointed." The scripture says, "They that have Godly wisdom shall be sought after." I walked in a measure of wisdom and the investigator was so impressed that he said I had wisdom beyond my years. I had the Ancient of Days living and governing my life by the wisdom of God. His wisdom can make a nobody like me look like somebody. He said He would take the foolish things of the world and confound the wise. I am a Foolish Thing; Glory!

I Survived

Now I don't believe they discriminated against me because I was Black, I believed they discriminated against me because I wasn't white.

Corporate America: They Had A Plot But God Had A Plan

I survived racial slurs, being the brunt of all jokes, and comments were made each time I changed my hairstyle. There were two other Hispanic girls that would change their hair color as much as I changed my hairstyle; however, the negative comments were not made about them. These two girls would come to my desk and ask me if their hair looked ok, because they were also afraid of being attacked, after witnessing me contstantly being attacked. Jealousy is as cruel as racism an as deadly as the grave.

I survived this by being patient. "There is a time to speak and a time to be silent." You remember the old cliché, "Give them enough rope and they will hang themselves." Well, they hung themselves; they began by playing mind games. I would greet them and no one would return a greeting all morning; however, after lunch they all would come by my desk and say good afternoon and I would speak back to them and then sit at my desk wondering if I had imagined that they all had not spoken to me earlier. They were trying to make me complain to others so that they could build a case that I was paranoid or over sensitive. I survived by being quiet and not saying anything to anybody about these mind games. They would roll their eyes at me or look at me with a very intimidating stare. I would ask my fellow employees did they see how the manager looked at me and the employees would immediately turn away from me. The Spirit said to me, *"The employees don't know if you don't say anything so stop giving this devil more power."* When the managers would go into one office and huddle and all signs were pointing at me, I would pray silently, "Lord, if this is forming against me, you said that they would come together against me one way and they would flee seven ways."

Prayer is a powerful strategy to use at your desk. This strategy will divide and conquer your enemy; if God be for me, He is more than the whole world against me. Now someone is saying with all these maneuvers going on. How can you do your job? I do my job effectively as a employee when I have to be a marriage counselor, a lawyer, a healer, an intercessor, and a solider in hand to hand combat all day long because I learned how to become all things to all men that I might win some. What I am sharing with you is something you could not have learned in the greatest university, or the most profound college, neither Moorehouse nor Howard University has a curriculum that could train you for what I have revealed to you in this book. As a matter of fact, what I

Corporate America: They Had A Plot But God Had A Plan have revealed in this book is really the prerequisite that will make you or break you, and this can only come through experience. *Experience, she is the best teacher.* You don't have the time to repeat a course now because time is running out. I can give you over 8 years of prepping and training through my experiences. If you ignore all this knowledge you won't survive; neither would I have survived if it weren't for the Lord on my side.

I stopped informing the employees what the managers were doing to me, what they were saying to me, and how the managers were looking at me. In this way I stopped giving management strength to execute my demise. This new strategy began to make the managers think that I was gaining favor with the employees, because the employees no longer isolated themselves from me when managers would enter the room. The Spirit said, *"Stop telling your co-workers because the co-workers don't even see them until you make them aware of what the managers are doing to you. Say, only what you want management to know in front of the office gossiper, because "a dog that will bring a bone will carry one."*

Betty Marie Knight
I Survived

    I survived by using strategy according to the word of God: "God said I will take the foolish things of the world to confound the wise." I listened to gospel tapes with my earphones the whole eight hours I was at work, while posting and placing vehicles into the web site. I listened to preaching which caused my faith to soar like never before. Now over half of the office listened to tapes with earphones; however, one of the vendors would come to my desk and ask me how I could listen to gospel all day long, and my response was, "easily." Little did they know I was being strengthened to fight the good fight of faith and to lay hold to eternal life. "Faith comes by hearing, and hearing by the word of God." When the managers realized that I was receiving strength by listening to the word of God on cassette, I was singled out again and told not to wear my earphones. This witch-hunt against me was actually building my case for me but I didn't know that then. They became obsessed with harassing and discriminating against me, it was if they had made a bet among themselves that they could make me quit or make me become insubordinate, break my spirit of joy, because I continued to laugh no matter what they did to me.

Since the employees no longer isolated themselves from me the managers were afraid that I was gaining authority, even more than they were. Strategy is the greatest survival plan in a Hostile Work Environment. Patience is a virtue because if you learn to wait, the professional mask will fall off and you will see things that impatient eyes can't see and hear things those impatient ears can't hear. Stay kind when they are mean, show love when you want to express hate; keep the peace in the midst of their confusion. When others see you hold out with the right frame of mind, then you are able to point someone to the Kingdom of God. Most of all do your work, that's what you are being paid for, even though this may not be what you are there for.

What we do for God is what we will be awarded for. As long as you remain Christlike, they are not aware of how much you know and you keep them in the dark while you remain in the light. When you are a light I found out people don't care how much you know, they trust you more when they see how much you care. God was able to build a case for me after I followed His instructions to the letter and learned to trust the navigator's heart when I could not see His hand. I was shaking like a victim but I was shining like a victor. God knew every move that they would make and He knew which road I would have to take. After He has tried me I shall come forth as pure gold; and he made me more than a conqueror.

I Survived

By remembering the tools you possess inside will assist you in surviving a hostile work environment. Your tools are the gifts and talents that God has placed in you. I have that gift of poetry and I used this gift to try to sow seeds of peace with my co-workers. This poem was used as evidence when I went to the EEOC to sue this company for discrimination. The gifts that God have placed in us are tools to implement purpose and destiny for a victorious outcome. My gift for poetry in the beginning was used to be a peacemaker and in the end served to be a part of my proof. God used this foolish thing called poetry to confound the mind of the wise.

Remember the Ten steps to Survive Working in a Hostile Work Environment:

1. **Greeting (Perception)**
2. **Ear to Hear**
3. **Know when to talk and when to keep silent**

4. Know who you are

5. Know what you are called to do

6. Strategy for working with toxic and difficult people

7. Using your tools (your gifts & talents)

8. Discern your atmosphere daily

9. Patience

10. Do your job and do it well

Perception

Iron Sharpens Iron

Some people see a glass half empty, while others see the same glass half full.

Perception

Two men in prison looking out of the same window

One man sees stars and the other man sees mud.

Perception

One race will teach their child how to start their own business

While another race will teach their child how to get a job.

Perception

Some people bring out different things out of different people.

There are 3 kinds of people

1. *There are people who watch things happen.*
2. *There are people that say what happen.*
3. *There are people that make things happen.*

Betty's Bits: Perception• **immediate knowledge obtained (perception or deception)**
- A Tragedy or A Strategy
- Complete or Compete
- Skill or Will
- Tactical or Practical
- A Deal or A Steal
- Rejection, Direction or Protection-

Corporate America: They Had A Plot But God Had A Plan

- Providence or Coincidence
- Attitude or Altitude
- Critical or Critic
- Demotion of Promotion
- A Servant or A Slave

It is all in the way you see it.

Chapter 3

SIGNS THAT ALERT YOU TO RECOGNIZE UNFAIRNESS OR DISCRIMINATION

To be treated unfairly is not against the law. Life is unfair, look at the third world countries where Aids kills millions of people a day. Millions of children are starving. Hundreds of people lose their lives in car accidents every day. Yet many women and men have so much money it would take them three lifetimes to spend it all. There are some who don't have a dime, yet God is still just. Every race, creed, and color is affected by pain. Every race, creed, and color enjoys wealth; every race, creed, and color is affected by poverty. Yes, life can throw all of us a curve ball; what can help you is knowing how to play the game.

Corporate America: They Had A Plot But God Had A Plan

I read one of Myles Monroe's books about God's Glory. He explained how a bank teller is trained to detect a counterfeit. "When a bank teller is trained to detect a counterfeit, they are trained thoroughly by handling the genuine." I repeat bank tellers are not trained by recognizing a counterfeit; they are trained by recognizing the genuine. I found that so interesting that I went into *Bank of America* and spoke with a teller named Victor. I asked Victor, "Why are the tellers trained in that manner?" Victor informed me that the counterfeiter is constantly up-dating the counterfeit currency to make it look real. Victor said, "Mrs. Knight, once you know the real thing you can easily identify the fake." He also said that tellers constantly study the genuine, because the original can't be imitated or duplicated.

We as a black race know when we are violated by discrimination vs. unfairness. We have had to study this unlawful discrimination in its most extreme form—slavery since 1619. Laws were passed and laws are still being written because of it and against it. We as a black race have the training of a teller. Once you have had to study discrimination constantly and consistently, you can easily identify the counterfeit unfairness. Discrimination is the treating of some people better than others for an unfair reason. However, the discriminator is constantly updating his procedures on how to discriminate with the counterfeit of unfairness, with the counterfeit of bias, with the counterfeit of prejudice, and with the counterfeit of inconsistency. Bayard Ruston said, *"History is not an accident; history, is a choice."* I heard Jerry Dunphy, the news reporter, state: *"The way to make history is to write it."* My prayer is that I will make a statement in history like Martin Luther King, Rosa Parks, Jessie Jackson, and Harriet Tubman. Their stand in history came with a price and many, many sacrifices. Fairness is to be free of bias just, and honest. Title VII of the Civil Rights Act of 1964 and the Civil Rights Act of 1991 affirm us as individuals against employment discrimination based on race and color as well as on national origin, sex, or religion. Once we know what discrimination is we can easily identify the counterfeiters:

Other Source: The Bible says, *"When you try to resolve a problem, if they won't hear you then take a witness."* When I attended the Work Health Program under Kaiser Permanente, an eight-week training program to teach us how to deal with toxic people in authority, over us, they suggested that we become more assertive, not aggressive. Then I decided to practice the biblical principles by approaching these toxic people with a

Buddy System. The Buddy plan can work for you in Corporate America because your buddy can keep a dairy on things that are questionable and will also be a witness of acts of discrimination. Once you have tried to clear the air and the manager still won't listen and resolve the problem, you need a witness to whatever is being said and done to you.

Next you need an attitude adjustment—a "What do I have to lose?" attitude. This comes after you have done everything in your power to reconcile this situation. What do you have to lose? You are not sleeping at night, you are not eating, and you are taking this out on your husband, your children, your friends, the dog and the cat. Furthermore, you have stopped feeding the goldfish. Everybody is tired of hearing about the way you are being harassed at work. As a matter of fact, they have told you for at least 3 years that you have a lawsuit, but you are afraid because you have made mistakes. So what! You have compromised on your values. O.K. You have done wrong too; you have said wrong things too. I know, been there, done that. Even with all of that, all they had to do was fire you and tell you your services were no longer needed with their company. They have a right to terminate an employee for not doing her job. However, they do not have a right to violate your Civil Rights. What does my lunchtime off the clock have to do with their supervision? Managers telling employees not to talk with you, not to go to lunch with you, telling you when to pray and when not to pray. When did they cross the line? Was it when they told me to get my butt up and leave now? Or was it when a manager told another manager to kick my butt out of her office? Was it when I would change my hairstyle and co-workers made me the brunt of the jokes? You Be The Judge!

Betty's Bits: If you will add to your self-image courage, determination and unwavering faith in God you can overcome and become more than a conqueror.

Chapter 4

THEY HAD A PLOT BUT GOD HAD A PLAN

Where did they cross the line?

Think about when you first saw the ad for your job in the newspaper, or when your friend told you about that wonderful job at the company where she works. It read: Now Hiring! Full benefits; pay raise, no experience necessary, vacation with pay and $75,000 a year salary. You read that ad and thought to yourself, I have ten years of experience, "I want that job." Here's another example, you have a love for children and a love to teach children. So you go back to college, get that Bachelor's degree, and then Master's degree, and then you get those credentials for Special Education. Oh, did I mention that you're the mother of

7 children, 2 in college, and 3 in Jr. High, and 1 in elementary. We as women have to wear many hats. We are wives and lovers, doctors, lawyers, and Indian chiefs. Did I mention that you are now $65,000 in debt for your education and you've made numerous sacrifices that qualify you for this career? Now you have prepared yourself for Corporate America, not realizing that Corporate America is not prepared for you.

So you pull that black suit out of the closet, leave home about 6:50 A.M., and go to apply for that job in that new career that has such a promising future and your name written all over it. You arrive at 7:30 a.m. and everyone seems so nice and excited about the new kid on the block. You sign all the necessary papers.

You are now given the Employee Handbook. You look at the Table Of Contents very closely and this chapter catches your attention. There is an *At Will Clause* in the handbook. The At Will Clause releases the company from all procedures and obligations. Meaning: I can --- ---- ------- ------- ----- ------ AT WILL! You fill in the blank. This Employee Handbook states the rules we will play by; however they never sign the contract, they just write it, and they don't bother to tell us that the rules has changed. Just imagine what this country would be like if we had a say so in the rules; even though we are making the decisions and all the odds are stacked up against us, some kind of way we manage to come out ahead. Corporate America makes the rules up as they go. A lawyer gave me some free advice, he said, "We as employees need to write the rules when we apply for a job in Corporate America." Rule Number One: is CYOA - Cover Your Own Attitude.

So don't look to use this handbook in case of a problem with a manager. The Employee Handbook is used to protect the company only, not to protect you. The Civil Rights 1964 Amendments are used to protect you. The Civil Rights Acts of 1991, states that if Corporate America has intentionally discriminated against you, monetary damages are due. However, if you don't know your Civil Rights you will not know when your rights have been violated. You will not know if you are experiencing unfairness or discrimination. The *At Will Clause* leaves the employee in a no win situation. The *At Will Clause* will release the company from procedures that they have agreed to in black and white. We, as employees, have read and agreed we will govern ourselves by these rules, and stated these are the rules we are to follow. Remember, Policies and Procedures are two different things.

- **Policy** is like law. A course of action or a contract.
- **Procedure** is what the company is governed by. Act or manner of proceeding; method of conducting business. How you govern and set forth procedures that can be changed **"At Will."** **At Will** will affect all employees.

There are unspoken requests in Corporate America:

- **Unspoken Request** is a request that is not voiced with the mouth, but is revealed or expressed in body language.
- **Body Language** in Corporate America can alert other managers as to when to cross the line with an employee from unfairness to discrimination. Body language is a powerful tool, and can be used negatively or positively.
- **Inconsistency** is a hazardous procedure to practice in Corporate America because when you treat one employee one way and treat another employee another way, this could be discrimination. However it can be viewed as inconsistency.

"Corporate America lacks consistency." Whether in business, in a school or ministry, etc., individuals should always be treated the same. Whenever a person is singled out and treated in an offensive, hostile, or derogatory manner, this is discrimination. This is called a witch-hunt!

Betty's Bits: Suppose we ran the red lights and did not stop at stop signs, what we will have is chaos. Well, that's the way the At Will Clause is. The At Will Clause can change policies and procedures, therefore leaving the company with the ability to run the red lights, and skip the stop signs of liability for their actions, by making the rules up as they go. Please remember this when you agree to and sign a policy for employment, your signing does not negate or violate your Civil and Constitutional Rights.

Are You Experiencing Trouble in Corporate America?

My eight years in Corporate America gained me experience, through suffering, that raised my level of commitment to God.

THE PRESIDENTIAL ELECTION, THE TERRIOTIST ATTACKS ON THE TWIN TOWERS AND THE PENTAGON GAVE ME FURTHER INSIGHT INTO EVERYTHING I EXPERIENCED WHILE IN CORPORATE AMERICA.

These experiences triggered questions, and these questions gave birth to this book: "Corporate America They Had a Plot, but God had a Plan."

I am old enough to know that life is bound to find two people who have been touched by the same tragedies: My own tragedy caused me to cross the paths of many others. My doctor felt it would be helpful for me to learn to channel the pain into power. Some of us fight with words and some of us write. I used my light of knowledge to win the fight in Corporate America; I helped schoolteachers, project administrators, bankers, tellers, nurses, security guards, co-workers and more. Once you get entangled into the Corporate America Fabric of Success, you must become a little inhuman to stay in a place of authority.

People dream of better lives, better salaries and a better career with a bright future, and one week around toxic people can erase all of that. Please read on because this book will expose you and prepare you for what college, and university, training can't. But some people would beg to differ.

Life experiences bring you knowledge and self-awareness that you can bring to the table as your contribution to the world. What I experienced was definitely not an isolated case, but an insulting case. Insults played out on the dreams of men and women who have given their time, and sacrificed their characters, integrity to fulfill the American Dream. After receiving your education and entering into the job market of Corporate America you won't believe some of the things that are being looked at as unfairness when they are really discrimination. The price others have paid helped me stand up against toxic and difficult people. There are

Corporate America: They Had A Plot But God Had A Plan

people stationed to kick the corporate ladder from under you in every walk of life.

Well, this brings me to investigating the investigator. Discerning of spirit is difficult when the atmosphere is unfair, especially when harassment is used so skillfully and those who have the power to judge can't determine whether or not Corporate America has crossed the line.

In the education field, teachers are targeted because they have so much to lose. They have paid from 65,000 to 150,000 dollars for their education, they receive the lowest pay in the work force, and their lives are on the line, even more so because now we have elementary school snipers. To add insult to injury, their status will dictate the level of discrimination in the education field. Credentials and recommendations are needed to advance and if your superior is not favorable towards you, you have a fight on your hands.

Lawyer vs. Counselor - trust the counselor in you because he knows all things and how to make them work together for your good.

Betty's Bits: I made God the head of my life and He fights my battles through me.

Chapter 5

TEAM PLAYERS

This call is for the team players,

Yoked together as a team

When we learn to function together

As one human being.

Let us all work together, many, performing as one

You're the leg; I'm the arm,

Ok, now who's the lung?

That's my point exactly;

when needed, step to the plate.

When we function as a team

We all have a chance to be great.

Corporate America: They Had A Plot But God Had A Plan

Team players need to learn the mindset of mountain climbers. While climbing up a very high mountain, harnessed together with nothing but a rope, being focused on one goal and climbing in the same direction is vital. This concept is a little different than a basketball team concept, because this connection is life or death. Determining what kind of team player you would like to be a mountain climber vs. a basketball player, which team player you decide on will determine the level of sacrifices you are willing to make. Remember mountain climbers do not have room for an ego.

My intention was to build-up the people at work, because morale was very, very low. I started to take money out of my own pocket, and buy gifts for men and women; I bought purses, jewelry, scarves, neckties, wood knots and sweaters. I would give the employee a gift if he or she would become a team player. I was the Safety Coordinator and I had printed little cards with a personalized poem on them to give the employees that had helped another employee to complete their work. A few of the employees did not appreciate my spending my money for this company, and some stated I was a fool because they felt this company and the management were very ungrateful. I tried to explain that I was doing this to build the morale of the company, not for the managers of the company. I had to focus on the big picture to learn this lesson and then be released to write a book and help anyone that would ever be discriminated against. I would give them affirmation, and validation to take that stand. Some of the employees were faithful and loyal to this company for over 24 years, and had not received any pay raises or good evaluations, or even simple words of encouragement, like "Good Job." One twenty-four year veteran of Ben's company told me, out of his own mouth, that he only made $7.00 per hour. In fact, in this man's testimony, I saw loyalty did not matter to this company. Also, if they could do this to a 24-year veteran, surely, I would not have a snowball's chance in hell here. I was harassed by co-workers for over a year and looked upon as the least of the employees because of my position as a file clerk. I used the poem "Team Player" to add to my paper trail. I presented two poems, "Crowning Beauties" and "Team Players" to the CEO of the company. I'm reminded of the stories in the slavery days when the slaves would be in the fields daily plowing, plucking or picking cotton and they figured out a way to communicate without the slave master understanding. Slaves used "coded songs" to

Corporate America: They Had A Plot But God Had A Plan
communicate to one another that a meeting would be held by the "Old Campground" or when an escape had been planned. The song "Steal Away" would lead God's people to freedom. Having your humanity always questioned, having your potential misunderstood is exactly what our ancestors faced over hundreds of years. Imagine all of this because of the color of your skin. Well, these two poems were "coded poems" that I presented to the CEO and the co-workers to try to put a stop to discrimination and harassment that I endured well over 7 years. This felt just like slavery and with cruel Task Masters!

To help me stay focused, and not get discouraged during this period of time, I put up a plaque that said, "My Present Position is not an Indication of my Future Potential."

Betty's Bits: There are two highly visible blacks in President Bush's Cabinet. Colon Powell and Condoleezza Rice. Just because they are visible does not mean that we have arrived. The very fact that we can name only two, the very fact that Denzel Washington and Halle Berry were the first awarded Best Actress/Actor Academy Award winners in 75 years, the very fact that we have never had a black President, not to mention a black Vice President, reveals that we have not yet arrived. If we are still using the word "first" then we have not come to far, but keep marching.

Once it becomes public knowledge that discrimination is sticking out where it can no longer be hidden, then a token is released for something that's been well overdue and even more well-deserved.

Betty Marie Knight

"My Present Position is not an Indication of my Future Potential," was coined by Reverend Mark Cinnrona. His words gave me the courage to fight, because I had the revelation. On this plaque I placed four pictures of myself at each corner with my own designs. Because I had to remember, "This Was Not It, I was Passing Through." Some employees had lost hope and heart because to some this was it. (Lord Help Us) At this moment if I had looked at the little picture I would have quit or been fired. I saw people in authority in bondage. It was like Egypt and the Children of Israel after being slaves for over 400 years. God said, *"Betty, I have heard the cry of my people, go tell Pharaoh to let my people go."*

Corporate America, "Let God's People Go."

Here are signs to help you tell Discrimination from Unfairness.

- Unfairness is not against the law, because life is not fair. Unfairness does not care what color you are, where you live, what car you drive, or how much money you make. Unfairness can find its way to you, regardless of race, or status. Unfairness is practiced in all walks of life. One man can see a glass half empty and the other man can see the same glass half full, meaning it can be the way you perceive a thing.
- Discrimination is so very subtle that if you are not knowledgeable of discrimination you will overlook it. As long as African American's choose to look on

Corporate America: They Had A Plot But God Had A Plan discrimination/harassment as an inconvenience most will not recognize it. As long as Non White/White America looks at discrimination as an on-going irritation most will choose not to recognize it. As long as we all choose to look at discrimination as either as an on-going irritations or as an inconvenience the **violations will continue.** These are **violations** not irritations!

Corporate America, "Remember, God has a set time when He will send a woman, or a man, boy or girl to expose and bring to the light whatever is in the dark!"

Diary: As an employee I could have made my walk in courts much easier if I had kept a better file on the company. When you write your grievances, write them in good_faith, honesty is the best policy.

I survived in this hostile work environment first because I was filled with the precious Holy Ghost. Secondly, God had sent me there to be a light to save souls and for His Glory. Thirdly, He wanted to teach me "that no weapon formed against me shall prosper, and every tongue that rises up against me shall be judged." There's a manager that I prayed for a year, her husband had left her for another woman. After we touched and agreed for almost a year in prayer, the Lord touched her husband's heart and he returned home to his wife. She came to me on a Monday morning and told me to come to her office. She informed me that this is not business this is personal. I had faced many challenges in this area so when she said the Lord kept giving her my name the Sunday after her husband left, I believed that what she said was true, because before that day we had only said hello and goodbye to each other on a few occasions. Once her husband returned home she became haughty and very unfriendly with me. Within six months he decided that he didn't want to stay so he went back to the other woman. This manager began to demand my time at home as well as at work, morning, noon, and night. The Spirit of the Lord said to me, "Do not pray with her about this any more." Now I was a little hesitant to obey this command because I saw this woman cruelly hurt by other employees, due to her marital status. You know what they say, "Hell Hath No Fury Like a Woman Scorned." I stopped returning her calls and she wrote me up and had another manager write me up as well, while she watched with a condescending look, as if to say, "You better get in gear." I was reminding God that He was the one who got me into this trouble so I was depending on Him to get me out. What do you do when you have done all you can? You just stand. God has a Purpose and God has a Plan. You just stand. I could hear Donnie McClurkin's song over and over in my heart and in my mind. I had to stand from April 1999 until March 2001. I endured write-ups for excessive phone use; write-ups for keypunch errors and unauthorized service; sexual advances; derogatory slurs and remarks; no pay for vacation days; harassment; retaliation—all because I obey God. Yet, I survived.

Crossing the Line

In Corporate America when they cross the line they use anything and anybody to win. Solomon states in Ecclesiastes 3 that God is also able to use anything and anyone for the fulfillment of His purpose. Remember all is fair in love and war. There is a time for everything. The question is, "What Time Is It?" What time is it when a friend who is a key witness has conveniently forgot a key part of her testimony? Yet you have her testimony in writing, what do you do? You must search your heart and know the time: God uses anything and anyone. There is a time to love, a time to hate, a time to lose, and a time to win. Trust God because He knows the End as well as the Beginning.

Boundaries: A line or limit where some things, such as a country, come to an end. Boundaries are used for your own protection. Set them in every area of your life.

Cross The Line: In any relationship there are boundaries—in friendships, in marriages, in the workplace, among believers, among families, etc. When boundaries are crossed, breaches form in relationships—breach's that may never heal. There is an old proverb that says, "It is easier to win a city than it is a man that's offended. Even while driving, crossing the line is a violation and remember an accident is bound to happen!"

Betty's Bits: Friendships are destroyed for crossing the line, marriages end in divorces for crossing the line, discrimination in the workplace means you have crossed the line, when believers walk in unforgiveness they have crossed the line, families cross the line when they can't honor the wishes of the deceased members. What I'm saying is this, get everything in writing because what people conveniently forget can be confidently restored, if written in black and white.

Chapter 6

CULTURAL DIVERSITIES

CROWNING BEAUTIES

Crowning Beauties is a Fan Club,

Anyone can join our team

There is only one qualification; you must be kind, not mean,

We build up one another always with encouraging words

Our focus is on the inside, regardless of what you've heard.

We all are individuals; variety is the spice of life;

Crowning Beauties are also gifted

There's no place for envy or strife.

If you see one you better recognize

They will not slack their duties

Their job description is a part of them;

That's How to Recognize a Crowning Beauty!

Cultural differences must be respected in Corporate America if we are to see reconciliation among the different races of people. We all need one another; I had to learn this at a very early age. My grandmother, Roberta, was not well educated. So a year before Booker T. Washington High School was closing its doors, the black students were progressing to receive a better education in the white school. Segregation was to be ended in Craighead County, my brothers and sisters had to face integration all alone. I learned back in 1963-64 what others have yet to embrace in 2002. We are all different on the outside and so much alike on the inside, we just have a different flavor and a different way of expressing it. There is a proverb that says, "Two can't walk together except they agree." Whenever we find a person to walk through life and agree, we have found someone special, especially when we can agree to disagree.

Well, in 1963-64, the law to stop segregation was passed and because my grandmother was not familiar with the process, she made my brothers Jimmy Ray, Peter and Terry, and myself, attend the white schools a year early. To make matters worse, because of our age differences we were placed at different white schools. It would have been much easier for us all to handle such

Corporate America: They Had A Plot But God Had A Plan

a great culture shock if were in the same school to support one another. So here we are in these white schools, by ourselves, with no support. My grandmother was a maid for a rich white family. Roberta while watching the news at work would overhear her boss in a conversation on integration. She had enough insight to know that segregation would one day prove to be no better for us than slavery was. Roberta knew that if her grandchildren could receive this opportunity, they would have a greater chance at owning rather than renting, starting a company rather than getting a job. When she explained it to us, we told her that segregation would be ending the following year. However, once her mind was set she could not be persuaded any other way. What I know now is this, she was trying to give us a head start in bettering our chances in Corporate America because she had to earn her living as a maid.

Betty's Bits: I used the poem *Crowning Beauties* to begin my paper trail to reveal the kinds of harassment I was under and enduring daily.

Cultural Diversities
Being black in the Workplace

There were times I really needed a word of encouragement while enduring the harassment and discrimination. There were days when e-mail was my only source of strength and comfort. So I would like to take this opportunity and thank all the e-mail supporters that encouraged, strengthened, comforted and gave me hope. Thank you to family members, friends and even foe. We all need a word of encouragement every now and then. That's why the concept of being a team player is an awesome one. You can get much more out of anyone if you give them a little TLC.

It was after I read this e-mail I knew I had to add it.

Subject: Being Black In the Workplace of America

1. They take my kindness for weakness.
2. They take my silence for speechless.
3. They consider my uniqueness strange.
4. They call my language slang.
5. They see my confidence as conceit.
6. They see my mistakes as defeat.
7. They minimize my intelligence to potential.

8. They consider my success accidental.

9. My questions mean I'm unaware.

10. My advancement is somehow unfair.

11. Any praise is preferential treatment.

12. To voice concern is discontentment.

13. Stand up for myself, too defensive.

14. If I don't trust them, I'm too apprehensive.

15. I'm defiant I separate.

16. I'm fake if I assimilate.

17. Yet, I undergo workplace hate. (Haters)

18. My character is constantly under attack.

19. Pride for my race makes me "TOO BLACK."

20. Yet, I can only be me.

21. And, who am I, you might ask?

22. I am a strong, black woman who stands on the backs of my ancestors achievements, pride, dignity, and respect, which lets the workplace in America know that I not only possess the ability to play by the rules, but I can make them as well.

Betty's Bits: A flatterer will say in front of your face what he/she will not say behind your back. An a Encourager will say behind your back what she/he has said to your face. Remember this.

Betty Marie Knight

A rule is a statement or principle that controls behavior or action:

The act or power of governing:

Rules

1) Think - it's not strange that I have addressed this unjust matter.

2) Listen - to me as an encourager and not a flatterer.

3) Discrimination - is a no-no, so let's just quit.

4) Put away - stereotypes and dispel the myths.

5) Stop - harassing one another under the mask of being harmonious

6) Stop - mixing and ignoring things that you know are erroneous.

7) Stop - contradicting the Constitution and our Civil Rights.

8) Listen - many men and women gave their lives to win this fight.

9) Think - the grass is not always greener it can be artificial turf.

10) Listen - "All men are created equal," God Almighty stated men's worth!

Segregation means to set apart from the rest.

From Segregation to Integration

At a very young age
I was able to see
Cultural diversities
Confronting me

I was placed in a school
With faces I did not know
Blonde hair and blue eyes
Different color for "sho"

They did not play with me
Because my skin was too dark
I felt segregation
Right from the start

I was just a child
That did not understand
Why this great necessity was upon me
Instead of a grown man

What I experienced
Was stares and isolation?
Because I was thrown
from segregation into integration.

Today I wonder was this really worse?
From integration to Discrimination
Disguised as a curse
A childlike faith in God
One day would bring restoration
Educate, Corporate America this is the Revelation.

Betty's Bits: As young as I was I could SEE all the things that were being done to me. Now I would like for you to see segregation through the eyes of an 8-year-old black girl that had no say. Even as a mature woman it's still being done a different way. Only now I have a voice.

Chapter 7

THE SECRECT CORPORATE AMERICA DOES NOT WANT YOU TO KNOW!

Open Door Policy - (1) a recognized right to admittance; freedom of acceptance. (2) A policy giving opportunity for commercial relations with a country to all nations on equal terms. (As defined by Webster Dictionary.)

Why are we afraid to exercise this right and walk into an open door? Use the Open Door to close the door on Discrimination. Go to the top CEO of the company. Some may say this is career suicide; however, emotionally and mentally you are almost dead anyway. Some one in authority has to be made aware of the discriminatory acts before the company can be held accountable.

Open Door Policy: This is the best of all policies, but everyone is afraid to go through it. I asked you earlier what you had to lose. Once you open this door, you have crossed the line that management prays no employee will have the guts to cross. The open door policy can obtain you an audience with the CEO, the President of the company! He or she is the Top Person in Charge. This is the secret weapon Corporate America does not want us to know. If we continue to close a door that is open to us, we will continue to aid in the violations of our Civil Rights. Once you go to the CEO, he or she is made aware of the harassment and discrimination and if he or she fails to rectify it, this is no longer your concern; it is the CEO's problem. Once the CEO knows the situation, the company is liable for what his management staff is doing; this is called "accountability!" Make the President accountable for failing to place qualified people in charge in his company.

Whatever the management does negatively from that point forward is called "retaliation!" This is exactly what you want to do, is make the CEO, the President of the company, aware of everything. Don't hold back anything—tell it all. The harassment, the sexual advances, the slurs, the manager that continues to use scornful looks to intimidate you. Once the CEO is aware of the discrimination and fails to correct this, if you are fired afterward, then you pull in the EEOC. Now you are leaving on your terms and not on their terms, knowing that all things are working together for your good. You have done the best job you can do, you have kept a personal file on the company (your diary), you have written everything in good faith, you have a buddy system that has supported you who will now also become your witnesses for you in a lawsuit, now you are ready for whatever comes next. Remember to go into the personnel office and check your file periodically because things will be placed in your file to help substantiate their grounds for termination. Anything placed in your personnel file unsigned is against the law. God has always sent the unqualified to speak to the CEO. Ask Moses: God doesn't call the qualified; God qualifies the called.

Betty's Bits: Fear is on its post. Fear has its assignment so that you will never use this open door policy. If fear is invading your very atmosphere now, this is evidence that the secret is out. Fear has torment and fear is designed to make you lose focus, retreat and lose hope. The secret is here... open door and accountability...according to John 10:1-18...God is the open door and accountable to no one.

SOS - in most cases if an employee files a Workmen's Compensation claim the claim will nullify the civil rights lawsuit. Definitely, if not handled very sensitively. E.g. if the Workmen's Compensation claim is dealt with regarding internal issues instead of psychological issues this becomes very sensitive. Workmen's Compensation insurance can/will quote Civil Rights issues that are Federal - make sure an attorney is aware of this - **the secret is out!**

Chapter 8

SETUPS

There is a movie coming out soon called *ENOUGH* staring Jennifer Lopez. I saw the preview on channel seven in between commercials. This movie captured my attention because it concerned a husband abusing his wife physically. The wife learns how to protect herself by practicing self-defense. In this movie the husband is killed while beating his wife, and this question is asked, "Was it murder or self-defense?" Whenever you're left asking yourself the question, was I violated? Look deep within because something hidden is about to come to the light. In this situation there is always a very thin line. When a person is shot and killed while breaking into someone's home, if they are killed in the house it is considered self-defense. However, if the person is killed while climbing out of the window of the house, is it murder or self-defense? Now you be the judge!

Remember, setups come in many shapes and many fashions. The good guy/bad guy ploy is a staple in Corporate America. One of these corporate heads will appear very nice, and the other will appear mean, and when they are caught practicing unlawful procedures, the nice one will step up to the plate and serve manipulation for an appetizer and reverse psychology for dessert they will try to make you feel guilty if you go through with a lawsuit. The good guy will manipulate you and your feelings so that you will not file charges. I saw this practice used on men as well as women, and employees have said repeatedly, "If it weren't for Sandy I would sue this company." Sometimes Sandy was very much a part of the setup and manipulating everything from behind the scenes.

Remember, you are not obligated to sign a written warning, and you can always make comments about the allegations that Corporate America has written up. The Setup is used skillfully on innocent and naive employees. A manager examines the employee to determine who will take the fall or be the scapegoat for a violation that management failed to stay on top of. That's why the Civil Rights Act of 1991 was written—for the employee that can prove intentional employment discrimination.

Not in Good Faith - This could be a labor code violations, as well as false representation of your character and integrity.

Beep-beep - This is one of the most undermining practices among co-workers, and managers that I have witnessed. It is the sound made when co-workers intentionally throw each other under the bus. For example, once while in a meeting with department heads the supervisors' actions or decisions were questioned. The supervisors were left answering questions that could have been viewed as dishonest. This practice builds an offensive atmosphere of disloyalty among workers. If those in charge of management do not address this, if they are allowed to continue, it divides co-workers, supervisors, and managers. Morale will be at an all-time low. Productivity will also be low because the atmosphere is filled with hostility. "A house divided against itself cannot stand." Different strokes for different folks.

Setups: Reminders are placed on the computer concerning 401Ks. If the company is not pleased with an employee who is nearing his 5th year of employment, for whatever reason,

Corporate America: They Had A Plot But God Had A Plan

reminders will alert management that the employee is about to become vested so the termination process is put in action.

Railroad: This is when the company will place you and other employees in another department without any training and then do what we call downsizing the company. You have invested 8 years and you receive a letter that your services are no longer necessary. After you take a notice you notice that it is only one ethic out of four that receives these letter.

As an Inventory Controller, I had to pick up inventory on certain vehicles. I had to travel to an off-site building. The white employees who went off-site were able to use a company vehicle. However, when the blacks would ask for company vehicles confusion would always occur. A black assistant manager told me that it would be better if I used my own car to go over to the off-site building. What he didn't know was that I had only enough gas to return home. Well, I was going to rock this boat. "Different strokes for different folks." There were white DMV clerks that were given a car each time they had to go off-site and they were not being told not to use the company's car for company business on company's time.

Cut Out: This is when you are working 40 hours a week and doing a good job but are not accepted by co-workers, or are disliked by a manager. Therefore a 40-hour week is turned into a 30-hour week. Then a 30-hour week is turned into a 20-hour week, and if you can't live on a 40-hour week paycheck you certainly can't survive on a 10-hour week. This is called "Cut Up to Cut Out!"

Leave a paper trail, each time your Civil Rights are violated and you are harassed/discriminated against by those in authority. Leave the paper trail; once you go and make someone in authority aware of the violation, leave another paper trail. This is to cover your back and also to cover your butt.

Betty's Bits: There is a thin line between love and hate, self-defense and murder, unfairness and discrimination. However, our Constitutional and Civil Rights helps us gauge the gray areas, and determine where and when Corporate America has crossed the thin line. Having the wisdom of God will enlighten us and help us keep everything decent and in order.

Examples for Keeping a Diary

A black assistant manager had been with a certain company for some 14 years and 6 months. When the white manager resigns, everyone knows the black assistant manager can keep the department running smoothly for at least 9 months. He is qualified for the position as manager; however, he is never given the position as manager. He is qualified to train white men as managers and help prepare them for the job he is already prepared for. During this 9-month period he didn't receive a pay increase, nor an incentive, or bonus, or even praise for a job well done! RED LIGHT! DISCRIMINATION!

Let's say you go way over the quota set in sales every week and you are causing the company to pay you a lot of money. Since you are on that rising pay rate, you are placed into a manager position. You need a team to work with you to make the new quota set for this new position. You see the team of men and women working under you are not excited about a black man or black woman now in charge of them. So they don't put their best foot forward, and productivity goes way down. Or maybe the team you have now is not as strong in sales as you are. As a matter of fact, they have given you all the weak salesmen and women so that you are demoted back to a salesman, and now you have to rebuild your clientele in order to make the money you were once making before you were given a promotion that you did not ask for. This is done for two reasons—so that it cannot be said that blacks are not managers (a crafty move that keeps us from drawing the race card) and because it blocks black salesmen and saleswomen from making the big bucks in sales. RED LIGHT! DISCRIMINATION!

Unlawful Harassment on the basis of race and/or color violates Title VII. Ethnic slurs, racial "jokes," offensive or derogatory comments, or other verbal or physical conduct based on an individual's race/color, constitutes unlawful harassment if the conduct creates an intimidating, hostile, or offensive working environment, or interferes with the individual's work performance. Harassment is done with malice and reckless intention, and violates your Civil Rights, which were ensured in the 1964 Civil Rights Act. Once those in authority place you in this box, and you step over where they have set your boundary, they become threatened by your very existence. The reason why all hell breaks loose when you walk into a room is because men love darkness rather than light, for their deeds are evil. You know within yourself that you haven't done anything to anyone to warrant this kind of abuse, and you find yourself building a great complex problem and you are wondering what's wrong with me. There's nothing wrong with you, there's something right

Corporate America: They Had A Plot But God Had A Plan

with you. When you place a black man in a manager position just to be the token, and set him up to fail with a weak team to avoid giving the appearance of discrimination, well, you have crossed the line. What I'm saying is this, be on alert when you are placed into a position of authority; you could be placed into this position because you are the token. Degradation is a counterfeit of disciplinary action, and it is hitting below the belt. It is very degrading to place a person in a head position and kick the corporate ladder from under him to keep from being sued.

Remember the movie "Men of Honor?" This black man was well-qualified, should I say over-qualified, to be a Master Diver in the navy. However, prejudice disqualified him continually. Even after he dove into the ocean and saved one of his fellow divers, prejudice was so strong against him that they awarded another diver, a white diver, the badge of honor for saving the other man's life, even after all of his peers saw him leave the diver in the ocean for dead. The black man stayed in the water until the diver was able to return up on deck. A token white man was used to keep from awarding the right man the right award because he was black. After that, the black man gained the respect of his fellow officers, his colleagues, his comrades, and proved that he was a man of honor.

Harassment and Discrimination have been hard to prove in courts of law up until now. It's like the man in the movie "Hollow Man." This invisible man was violating friends, women, and his colleagues, and threatening their careers and finally their lives. The project leader, Sebastian, volunteered himself as the guinea pig for this project; he was not given permission by those in authority over this special team because the formula had not been tested enough to use on humans. Consuming the fluid made the physical anatomy invisible. This team had special glasses to see Sebastian and knew what he was doing, even though he was invisible. That's the way discrimination is to those who don't have eyes to see. In this movie, one of the women on the project used blood to make the hollow man's footsteps visible. To everyone that believes in the power of the blood, use the blood to make discrimination visible. Once they put a face and a body on the Hollow Man, they were able to expose him and eventually kill him. That is the way harassment and discrimination are, once you uncover them, you must destroy them! Red Light! Discrimination!

Corporate America: They Had A Plot But God Had A Plan

When you walk out of the norm, you will shake things up. People fear change, and people who can bring about a change are threats to those in authority in every walk of life. Fear is a **F**alse **E**vidence **A**ppearing **R**eal. I heard a friend say this and God removed all my fears by forcing me to face them. He delivered me from them all. Patience is a great tool to use in Corporate America. "Let patience have her perfect work that you may be full and complete, lacking nothing." Remember, the person who is greatly attacked is the person that has submitted and allowed their light to shine before men through the storm. God gave me orders for seven years in Corporate America, to go into this company with the Spirit of Jeremiah. God set Jeremiah over the nations and over the kingdoms to root up, and to pull down, destroy and to build and to plant. After I finished my assignment, God took me off that job and set me down for one year to heal and use my experiences and let me write about it. While I was on Sabbatical leave that year, he healed me spiritually, physically, mentally, emotionally, and yes, financially. I was financially blessed because I took a stand that others were afraid to take. I reaped the harvest that other men sowed because they were too fearful to pluck it up.

Betty Marie Knight

Betty's Bits: Remember! With the right tools you can survive a hostile work environment! And this is how you know that you have survived. Make the company write a new Employee Handbook, at least make them add a couple of new chapters.

Gathering Evidence

After watching television, and witnessing violations in every walk of life, I realized that sharing with people experiencing the same problems, with black men and black women who have fought, sacrificed, and even died for, these civil rights, I had no choice but to share my insight.

We have all heard these statements before: "If it's not in writing then it has not been said." "Get it in black and white." What do you do when a video camera, witnesses, and evidence are presented and the violator is allowed to go free? Even with all of that evidence, a decision can still be rendered that is not in your favor. What do you do? Well, I had to look to someone greater and bigger than you and me.

Before you take this stand make sure that you are up for the fight, several challenges and obstacles will arises, such as unfairness.

Corporate America: They Had A Plot But God Had A Plan

It was unfairness like this that caused the unrest in Los Angeles in 1964, the boycott in Montgomery, the Underground Railroad, and the Rodney King beating. It's made America realize that racial profiling is becoming America's pastime.

*Red Light: When a credible witness is not called in to give her deposition in front of the investigator and the company's lawyer, believe you me, unfair play is somewhere in the game. The question now is whom is the unfair play being initiated by? The investigator who is on your side (?) or the company's lawyer who the charge is against? Keep this in mind—*It's the details that make the difference!*

* Remember, in the multitude of counsel there is safety! *

*What is it going to take to see that our country needs reformation, restitutions, reciprocity, resolutions, and most of all a relationship, if we are to really become: ONE NATION UNDER GOD WITH LIBERTY AND JUSTICE FOR ALL!

Here I am suffering Post Traumatic Stress Disorder for over 3 years and now America is about to witness and suffer what I had under the disguise of discrimination.

Nine-One-One

September 11, 2001, was the day an assault was launched on America.

9-1-1 is symbolic emergency call to the body of Christ. We were not ready in the church, and we were not ready in Washington, to aid the people during this crisis.

Washington Security Intelligent was relaxed and unaware of what was going on. I believe this terrorist had not only manifesting in the Natural it had already manifested in the Spirit and I had been under terrorist attack in Corporate America. This is a 9-1-1 call to the Body of Christ, wake up the Sleeping Giant.

Stand! After having done all to stand—Stand!

A letter to Mr. Grant

Mr. Grant, I listened to your ministry on TBN on Sept. 3rd, 2001, which was Labor Day. It confirmed so much of what I have personally witnessed. I have written three books, on Spiritual Warfare. God took me through a total of 23 years on instinct and strategic warfare drills so that I could receive spiritual warfare strategic, SIGII.

Corporate America: They Had A Plot But God Had A Plan
With each lesson I learned, I wrote a poem or found a message in my spirit that I could comfort and console others who were going through what I was going through.

These three books, I believe have been sent to the kingdom for such a time as this. After watching this strategic move of the devil sent through bin Laden, I knew if I could sound the alarm and not sleep like those in government did, others will be aware of the devil and his devices.

Revelation 2:12-13, "AND TO THE ANGEL OF THE CHURCH IN PERGAMOS WRITE THESE THINGS SAITH HE WHICH HATH THE SHARP SWORD WITH TWO EDGES. I KNOW THY WORKS, AND WHERE THOU DWELLEST EVEN WHERE SATAN'S SEAT IS: AND THOU HOLDEST FAST MY FAITH, EVEN IN THOSE DAYS WHEREIN ANTIPAS WAS MY FAITHFUL MARTYR, WHO WAS SLAIN AMONG YOU, WHERE SATAN DWELLETH."

These three books are to alert the body of Christ! To make known and bring elimination of satan's seat in the church, in Corporate America and in connubial relationships, to reveal strategic warfare on how to judge everybody around us, whether they are our friends or enemies by their level of support.

For the first eleven years of my 45 years of life, I faced struggles that I recognized were not normal for one so young, but I saw through prayer that changes could take place. Being from a small town in Jonesboro, Arkansas, trying to be a light in a predominately white community during the time of integration, I survived everything a poor black girl could. My grandmother, Roberta, and my grandfather, Russell Wise, raised me and instilled in me faith and prayer.

I have been training for 34 years in Spiritual Warfare. My second assignment was to the Church. Brotherly Love is the key that helped me to be neither barren nor unfruitful; the knowledge of our Lord Jesus Christ dwelling in me has helped me to see afar off. This brings me to the most important chapter in my book. This chapter is called the Birth of Love. Love, which caused me to deny myself, pick up my cross and follow Christ. I was in the Armed Forces, a dependent to my husband. While my husband was in the United States, I did not travel. But in 1976 my husband was stationed in Ashuffenburg, Germany, in the United States Army. I followed him there and learned warfare can be with those in authority over you. My husband's Drill Sergeant told him a snowball in hell would have a better chance than he would in his platoon.

Spiritual Perception was necessary in order to judge God faithful. I watched those in authority maneuver with the enlisted men and women that were strategically set to kick the foundation out from under them. The army, navy and the marines are not our true security; God is. Our trust should be in God. I saw God strategically position me to get the insight I needed to teach the Body of Christ how to Fight Spiritual Warfare.

This task was set to exercise my spiritual muscles, and discern the enemy whether inside or outside of the camp. Lieutenants or Generals used by the enemy is called a double agent, who will play both sides.

Betty's Bits: Remember, God uses locusts, frogs, and things like four lepers to win the battles. Surely, if He can use these things surely He could use me. If God be for you He is more than the whole world against you!

Chapter 9

CRUCIFIED CROSS EXPERIENCE

It was an experience on Easter Sunday morning, April 3rd 1988, that prepared me for what I had to endure in Corporate America. The isolation, negative remarks, condemnation, gossip form those in authority setting me up to fail, not sleeping and being filled with anxiety, yet I waited upon the Lord to renew my strength.

I had a crucified cross experience. God made St. John 14:1-6 illuminate in my Spirit that He was still in control, no matter what circumstances tried me. My husband was accused by a group like Pilate's and was marched through Kangaroo Court like Jesus. Since I am one with him, what they did unto him they did unto me. He was asked not to come to church the Saturday

Corporate America: They Had A Plot But God Had A Plan

night before Easter; just imagine not being allowed to go into God's house on Easter Sunday morning, the day you recognized as the most significant time of your existence.

That morning my mother was waiting for me to cross the street so that we could sit together in church. However, I knew what was awaiting me, I stooped down and began to pretend I was doing something so that she would go on ahead. She looked at me very strangely, however, I knew she would never understand that God had nothing to do with this kind of behavior that the saints were about to express to two very faithful, tithe-paying, offering-giving, ministers, Sunday School teachers, and Alto Team leaders. Betty's flesh died that Easter Sunday morning and this prepared me for Corporate America.

I began this love walk in 1988, a love walk that was noticed by this little Italian lady in Corporate America. On January 6th, 2001, I was given a 6-inch steel nail from the administrative assistant who saw me carry my cross through profound discrimination. That experience made me even more aware of God may not come when I want Him to come. But, He is right on time.

Now this brings me to the 2nd book "Corporate America." Some things I gave and some things I lost. Only God knows what that lesson cost. This was a 7-year lesson. God positioned me in a business office in Corporate America, and let me see naturally and spiritually how discrimination is practiced and legally accepted as unfairness. I denied myself, picked up my cross and followed Him through this suffering and dying out to my flesh. I know beyond any doubt, "No weapon formed against me shall prosper."

I stopped wrestling with flesh and blood. Because each time I allowed my flesh to pick the battleground, I lost. My brother worked for the U.S. Postal Service in Texas where he saw some employees get tired and shoot up a whole department. I saw some employees get demoted from a position that they were well qualified to fill. I saw some employees almost lose their minds because of the unfairness of those in authority over them. I saw some employees go out on stress and be afraid to return to Corporate America. This is one way to notice delegated authority—when you see Mickey Mouse turn into Mighty Mouse.

Who is the enemy? Discrimination! And how do we fight? By knowing our Civil Rights! In this book I describe delegated authority. Delegated authority is when a co-worker moves into a position not with title or the pay but the authority to assist and implement in delegating a plot. There is a time to speak and a time to keep silent; knowing when to speak is a weapon. Being aware of time as described in Ecclesiastes 3: 1-15 helped me gain insight to discern on a keen level how to navigate spiritually day to day. I learned to trust God to get me to my destination through Turbulence or Tail Wind. Trust God to see what I could not see; hear what I could not hear.

Eight hours a day, five days a week, Monday through Friday, not being able to prove anything, not having a grasp on anything, just trusting. Knowing God helped me suspend my intellect, my senses, to be a Light in this Dark, Dark place! I learned to decrease and allow God to increase. I learned to eavesdrop on the adversaries by listening to what they did and did not do, by what they would say and would not say.

I understood Paul when he was in jail in Rome and wrote the letters to encourage or inform the church while he himself was being persecuted. The Spirit of God ministered to me by His gifts while I was in this prison situation. The word of wisdom got me prepared for the future; the word of knowledge helped me prepare for all I was dealing with now. Discerning of spirit helped me to discern my co-workers, whether they were for me or against me. I also judged the enemy in them by their level of support. I saw managers become enemies. I saw co-workers become enemies. I stood alone, little did they know I had come this far by faith, and I knew the employees that pretended to be on my side. I knew if they were for me by the level of their support in front of management, while I was under attack. I understood that they feared retaliation for their jobs; however, I also knew if this was the time they had chosen to reveal what I knew was always in their hearts. When you get on my nerves that is my flesh, but when you vex me that is Spiritual and that would set off an alarm in my spirit and make me question whatever was going on around me.

I have learned to trust my Spirit because my Spirit was all I had, just as Paul learned to trust his Spirit, because he wrote over 3/4 of the New Testament while in prison.

I want you to know this insight cost me more than you will ever know. However I was willing and ready to pay the price. I counted up the cost; when God called me, He said, "Seek ye first the Kingdom of God and His righteousness and all these things will be added unto you." The rewards came from knowing that all things worked together for my good, because I loved Him, and I am one of the called according to His purpose. Believing will keep guilt and condemnation from plaguing your mind when those in authority are trying to make you feel incompetent.

God revealed to me through my tribulations in Corporate America that tribulation worketh patience, patience experience, experience hope, and hope maketh not ashamed.

I endured this trial as a burn victim does. There were many fiery darts of wickedness. Once you are burned, allowing the burn to air out promotes healing. Burns cannot heal when we allow them to be bandaged up. So get up and get busy, it is time to uncover those burns so your healing can begin. Uncover the pain and the violation by your words, positive words are therapeutic. Place yourself around people who are kind and loving, whether at home, or at a support group. Get around people who you know only want the best for you. I also compared this violation to as being raped. When a child is raped he/she is told by the rapist that this is his/her fault, and this is said so that the child will not reveal her rapist. The child is blamed and brained-washed while continually being violated. However, once you expose the rapist, the violation is discontinued. So Tell It!

Betty Marie Knight

I believe a molester best defines this violation of discrimination in a deeper sense because the rapist is forced sexual deception and the molester persecution with hostile intent of sexual force. This is when discrimination and harassment are running neck-and-neck.

Betty's Bits: Remember, you need a cross if you decide to die. "Vengeance is mine saith the Lord and I will repay." God did repay!

Chapter 10

KAISER PSYCHIATRIC CARE

Kaiser Psychiatric Care
I came to this program in pain & despair
You helped me gain much of what I lost
Only God knows what this lesson cost
Your education and experiences, added to your life
When you shared it with me, it helped to value my price
I started out feeling hopeless & in pain
It's Corporate America's loss
Listen, it was so much to gain
Some of us have discovered our purpose
I will fulfill my destiny
With a new determination
Because of the skills you shared with me.

Betty Marie Knight

Work Stress Program

I took a Work Health Program Class that Kaiser offered to employees that had been under severe attack in Corporate America. I learned about the Labor Laws. They also provided information on the procedure for filing a charge at the EEOC for discrimination. Other employees shared their experiences, and gave me insight as how to file a charge so that it would not be cast into the frivolous EEOC file. EEOC stands for the Equal Employment Opportunity Commission. In this class several of us came together and role-played the incidents so we would know how to prepare our case. We formed a support group that met on Saturdays and gave each other moral support to stand up for what we knew was right. Over the course of this 8-week program, I gained skills and insights that I have written in this book to help someone else who's been violated and lacks the skills to prove it. In this program there were approximately 85% blacks, 10% Hispanics, and about 5% white. The people from the U.S. Postal Service were very hostile with one another in this program; that the atmosphere get so volatile that they would have to leave the classroom. These were some very angry people that admitted they needed help.

If someone reads these books and learns from my pain, this will help me gain one of my rewards, because my pain is someone's gain.

Now this brings me to the chapter on connubial and relationships. I too was like Paul, I was in a prison situation. Spiritual warfare in relationships is designed to prevent unity and agreement. The enemy knows if there is agreement in any relationships, goals will be accomplished and the sky is the limit. Be not unequally yoked is a command, but we view it as a statement. A statement is just a suggestion, but a command is an order.

Being unequally yoked will stop any relationship from reaching their highest potential. Through each trial, through each test, through each lesson, we must evaluate our walk with God and with man.

The Scripture said Jesus learned obedience by His suffering. I learned obedience by my suffering. An emergency call to the sleeping giant, 9-1-1, please "Wake Up." I know this book will wake up those spiritual gifts that we have not sharpened by exercising them daily.

I know that these three books will expose the enemy, in every shape, form, and fashion. Jesus said He would not have us ignorant of Satan's devices, hatred, discord, and lies. For Satan cometh but to kill, steal, and destroy. Kill your reputation, steal your influences and destroy your hopes and dreams.

I have not only gone through; I have helped an educator become an over-comer. I have helped a corporate administrator become an over-comer. I have helped students become over-comers. I have helped relationships become over-comers. I received certificates, cards, and telephone calls from people in every walk of life who have over-come by the Blood of the Lamb and the Word of my Testimony.

I became even more determined after I heard T. D. Jakes teach on "Ten Commandments on Working in a Hostile Work Environment." I decided with his added knowledge, I needed to get the word out that would encourage people and share with them. This book will be a witness, in Jerusalem, Judea, Samaria and to the uttermost parts of the earth. I will get this knowledge into the hands and hearts of people who the enemy has played mind games with; he has made them almost believe that they are unbalanced. Now they can know beyond any shadow of doubt that the enemy's supply has just run out!

I had many people say thank you so very much for my response to this 9-1-1 in exposing Corporate America.

I feared Corporate America's legal system because this company that I worked for has included in its yearly budget money to allow them to get away with breaking Civil Rights laws and using managers to lie, cheat, and steal to win their cases. Their lawyers are at their beck and call 24/7 and I believed they were very well qualified. During the arbitrations I feared the date of the mediation between the company and myself; however, on that day I saw Corporate America slip and send the wrong lawyer for the job. Never send a boy to do a man-size job. On June 20, 2001 I had my day in court, which helped me to finally forgive and close this chapter.

So God chose the time and the place. Since I had to learn to wait upon the Lord, I only said four sentences, and I had the opportunity to stare at them the way they had done me for four years and they tried to intimidate me. But this time I stared back and they saw that I was no longer under their power. The mediator said, "I can tell this is not going to be resolved today. The hostility in this room is so thick that you can cut it with a knife." Their lawyer had fumbled enough for me to realize that I did have a fighting chance. The attorney forgot to inform the company that I was bringing a representative to the meditation. This mistake would prove to be very costly because my representative was not bound to client and attorney confidence.

I said openly, "I've witnessed this type of hostility for over 4 years," I again apologized for being late. I then stated, "If your lawyer failed to inform you of the procedure that's his fault."

From that moment there was no reason for me to fear them or their lawyers anymore. I knew that day that the ball was in my court. I had the strength of Shaq, I had the guts of Kobe, I had the 3-point shot of Fisher, and I had the tenacity of Fox. I saw myself as the MVP for everyone that had been discriminated against and lacked the guts to speak up, lacked the words to articulate it, lacked the tenacity to take a risk, lacked the confidence and the drive of Horry, who can take a shot under great pressure in the last seconds of the game. I had a great crowd of witnesses on the bench in heaven cheering me on. The Lakers are now two points behind and all the odds are against them, as they wrestle for the rebound at the Sacramento court in the 4th game of the

Corporate America: They Had A Plot But God Had A Plan

NBA playoffs. Well, that is how I felt after I heard the owner say that their lawyers had failed to inform the company as to who would be attending the mediation meeting with me. That opened the door for me to bring in a long time friend and prayer partner of 15 years for moral support. I felt that they had fumbled the ball and had accidentally hit it into my hand and I did what Horry did, Horry stood still and hit 3 points. Final score was 100-99. I knew 99 ½ wouldn't do. I stood still to see the salvation of the Lord.

My lawyer had called and said he would be late, but he never showed up. However, I had already confided in the lawyers of lawyers, J.C. I confided in a lawyer that's never lost a case, I had a judge that would grant me mercy, and I had a jury that would always hand down to me a verdict of not guilty. No, it's not Johnny Cochran it's Jesus Christ! Glory! I don't want to toot my own horn; however, I'm the kind of person that any winner would want on their team. I'm like Mike Bibby; all he can do is enhance the team; the Lakers should draft him. I am not arrogant neither am I proud, but I have paid the price to be confident that God who has begun this great work in me will perform it until the day of Christ Jesus. My grandmother would say to me, "It's a poor dog that won't wag its own tail."

I love to listen to the commentary while the Lakers play their games. The commentator told us that the night before the 6th game Kobe called Shaq around 2:00 in the morning and said, "I'm going to need you tomorrow night, let's make history." Kobe didn't say, "Let's win this game." No, Kobe saw the big picture: the big picture was let's make history" and the little picture was let's win the game and history is what they made. "If two shall touch and agree on anything," that principle will always work! The power of agreement is awesome!

The concept of being a team player is a good one; however, which kind of team player you are will determine the sacrifice that will have to be made. A mountain climber vs. a basketball player; you be the judge!

Here we are as a nation airing the largest car chase in history, and to add insult to injury we are in our 40th day without a president in office.

I was able to relate this experience to the terrorist attack on America. I believed bin Laden saw us air our dirty laundry one time too many on national T.V., chasing cars on every freeway in California from the 105 to the 605, from the 105 to the 405, from the 91 to the 110, and from the 10 to the 710. I could go on and

Corporate America: They Had A Plot But God Had A Plan

on, but this is how ridiculous we must have looked to the world. We will watch this until the person either runs out of gas and gets out of the car with their hands up, or are stopped by the police.

Then we aired the longest presidential election in history. This made people in certain areas look so foolish. We trusted the President and his cabinet; then on Election Day our voting polls revealed our President conspiring to use Democratic votes for Republican votes. This aired all over the nation for everyone to see. I believe the enemy saw that we felt secure and complacent, while they lived in terror every minute of the day. It was enough to plan, strategize, and scheme to let America see how the other countries live under terrorist attack almost every day of their lives, so September 11th manifested. We were 43 days into the attack, the stress was unbelievable. However, I felt if I had a platform I could have helped the nation deal with it because I had that experience under Corporate America. After my mediation with the companies' attorneys and seeing how they did not possess all the power that I thought they had, I overcame my ultimate fear.

Well, after my meeting with my company at the EEOC mediation, over 43 days, I was able to sleep all night without the help of Serzones—pills that relaxed my mind so I could sleep.

For three or four years, I had a preview of what America experienced on September 11th, 2001. Corporate America left me traumatized the same way the terrorists left America traumatized. I would not fly as of October 24, 2001. The airlines were suffering and we were all watching the mail, afraid of being exposed to anthrax. New York was still trying to get back to normal. There are flight attendants, pilots, firemen, fathers, mothers, and brothers, and sisters who will never fly again. That's the way the Transition is when it's time to return to Corporate America. You feel like you never want to return to the workforce since you know that no new laws have been written nor has there been a change of government.

Corporate America will have their lawyers do the dirty work and cover it up. Then the cover-up is called client-lawyer privilege. What confidentiality?

God Bless America

"There Is a Best seller In Me." I promised my readers that I would not forget to write. I promised as God revealed to me the injustices that are being practiced in Corporate America that I won't be like those in authority over the nation—caught sleeping.

Corporate America: They Had A Plot But God Had A Plan

I won't sleep on the job; I will make you aware of the tricks of the enemy. Be on alert! "Discrimination is still up and running."

I listened to Ray Charles sing "America, America, God shed His Grace on thee, and crowned thy good, with brotherhood, from sea to shining sea." I feel God shed His Grace on me and revealed through me simple knowledge to help put a face and a body on discrimination, to make it so visible that other laws will be written against it. Glory!

Betty's Bits: SOS for the next presidential election, don't be surprised if within two to three weeks of the voting, if over 50% of the polls are closed and new locations for voting polls are made known.

We are in the time that knowledge will fill the earth. The computer is definitely a manifestation of this. In the scripture Isaiah 45:2-3, "I will go before thee, and make the crooked places straight. I will break in pieces the gates of brass and cut in sunder the bars of iron. And I will give thee the treasures of darkness, and hidden riches of secret places, that thou mayest know that the LORD, WHICH CALLS THEE BY THY NAME, AND THE GOD OF ISAIAH." I believed that's what He did for me through this book. God revealed the treasures of darkness in discrimination in a way that has taken the covers off; and discrimination can never hide its head again. Glory!

Betty Marie Knight

THE PRIVATE INVESTIGATOR INVESTIGATES THE COUNSELOR

II Chronicles 26:5, "And he sought God in the day of Zechariah, who had understanding in the vision of God." "As long as he sought the Lord, God made him to prosper."

Have you seen the movie "The Green Mile?" John Koffee knew things by the "Word of Knowledge." Koffee learned how to operate his gift to such a level that he did not enjoy life on earth anymore. He knew things that others did not know.

When the investigator came to discuss the robbery he became more interested in the gift of discerning. He had breakfast with me at CoCos. He said to me, "You have been very helpful in bringing closure to this case." He encouraged me that I had a gift that would prove to be more powerful than I could ever imagine. He also informed me that he was going to talk to the owner, President and the Vice President of this company. He said, "I am going to tell them how much help you have been to me in this case. You better believe they will know all about you when I leave. How you 'flow in that gift.' I laughed and said, "to God be the glory."

Well, after this I know something positive was said about me because that's what made the managers call me into meetings for my insight on solving company problems. I had the judgment to judge? Was judgment to judge something that these people in authority lacked? The gifts in operation will bless you and others.

The private investigator and I bonded in the area of investigating. He learned a stronger awareness of his ability for what the world calls ESP. He affirmed and confirmed my gift by the questions he asked me. But there is a difference between my gift and ESP. "This gift will discern the thoughts and intents of the heart."

Advice for Lawyers and EEOC Investigators

Time can work for the suit or against it. I think all testimonies should be received as soon as possible. Waiting can be a tragedy as well as a strategy. Within a year so much can happen, people forget, or should I say they conveniently forget. People can move people can die. What I'm saying is things can happen that can place a suit in jeopardy. So get his or her testimonies as soon as possible while everyone involved is standing up, remembering!

Betty Marie Knight

What is the question that will eventually be asked?

"Ms. Knight could you be just a little paranoid?"

The Answer: "Absolutely Not! It was not paranoid! It was humiliation!

It was not paranoid! It was degradation. This is not paranoia! This is retaliation! This was not paranoia! This was discrimination!

There is an old Proverb that says, "Know ye how to answer every man for the hope that is within you."

Betty's Bits: Strategy used could be to get the accuser or plaintiff to give all of his/her testimony so that the company will know how to fight, or allow the investigator to use your evidence against you. Whatever you do, remember, I was able to use character witnesses because this company was determined to execute my demise at Christmas parties, company picnics, retirement parties, restaurant outings. I invited a friend or family member and the department heads/employees still displayed discriminatory practices towards me. I was able to use my family and friends as character witnesses.

Things I found Questionable that the EEOC Investigators Do:

1). Don't answer questions no one is asking!

2). Don't ask questions if you have already prepared the answer!

3). Don't ask the wrong question of the right witness!

4). Don't ask the right question of the wrong witness!

5). Don't interrupt the witnesses while they're giving their testimony. That strategy can twist their testimony.

Betty's Bits: "I don't remember it that way," is a nice, legal way to lie; however, if you do remember, withholding evidence is a Federal Offense: After I made it through the EEOC, I realized I needed my Dream Team—the Father, Son, and the Holy Ghost.

Red Herring* Please watch out for a red herring, I had this pulled on me so many times by the EEOC investigator, until I said to myself this feels like I'm still at the company that I was filing a charge against. I responded in such a way that the EEOC investigator looked at me and said, "Mrs. Knight, I don't want to sound like the devil's advocate." I replied, "Then why are you?" Oh yes, a red herring is a diversion or a distraction that takes you off of the course of your original thought. Depending on how skillful the person is in executing a red herring, they can have you on another subject entirely, asking you questions that you don't know how to answer. Now they really have you at a disadvantage because you have become unsure about what

Betty Marie Knight

you are saying, simply because you are discussing something you don't understand. This is where you lose confidence and begin to doubt yourself.

When you file a discrimination case at the EEOC, please remember that the *"details makes the difference."* It's not the EEOC, it is G O D!

Chapter 11

CIVIL VS. FEDERAL

Remember, the laws are written to protect the violator. Look, for example, at the O.J. Simpson trial, "the trial of the century." The law says, if there's reasonable doubt you must find O. J. Simpson not guilty. One member of the jury had reasonable doubt. Johnnie Cochran coined the familiar phrase at the end of the trial—"If it doesn't fit you must acquit." However, this evidence could not convict O. J. Simpson in the Federal Court. This same evidence did convict O. J. Simpson in a civil lawsuit for punitive damages. This is what helps a violator get away with murder in a court of law—reasonable doubt. The evidence that would not win in a Federal Court could still be used to prove that your Civil Rights have been violated. So whatever the EEOC cannot do, remember a Civil Rights Suit can. A Civil Rights Suit can defeat Corporate America if your Civil Rights have been truly violated.

Remember, Federal Law states a person is innocent if there is any reasonable doubt. However, in a civil lawsuit if there is ponderous of evidence, the company can be convicted of discrimination. Ponderous of Evidence means it holds great weight based on the information given, your Civil Rights were violated. If you have witnesses, keep a Journal/Diary of the day-to-day transactions of what was done and said, then continue to move forward. The EEOC should give you right to sue papers even if the EEOC cannot prove that you were violated. By federal law standards, you have the right to file a Civil Rights lawsuit. So file!

Betty's Bits: Remember, the Department of Fair Employment and Housing can be another option to file a discrimination charge for a quicker resolution.

Corporate America: They Had A Plot But God Had A Plan
From the Desk of

Betty Knight

To all of my readers, I hope that since you are now on page 93 and reading this letter, you have been helped, inspired, confirmed, assisted, enlightened, and motivated to pursue any goal, dream,

desire, or vision. You have within yourself everything you need to fulfill your dreams. Chapter 1-11 are full of power tools to help you reach your highest potential. Keep reading, your life will only get better with the concepts and principles I have revealed in this book. Stop by poetrydiva2003@yahoo.com and give me your thoughts about the first eleven chapters. Then finish the book and write your Senators, the Congress, yes, the President, until the laws are changed and we make our dent in history like our ancestors did.

Chapter 12

WHAT IFS

I would like to share excerpts from the *fact sheets* to help you see where and when discrimination/harassment is being practiced.

Sexual Harassment: The victim does not have to be the person harassed but could be anyone affected by the offensive conduct (third-party harassment). For example, when you (accidentally) witness a supervisor/co-worker having an affair. When you catch co-workers flirting with each other on several occasions. When you see her go past his office several times a day until he gets up from his seat and follows her down the stairs, sits across from her and flirts in the lunchroom. The third party should not be retaliated against because of what she/he witnessed.

Retaliation is commonly used, especially when both parties are married to someone else. The third party should not have to lose their job because of the supervisor/co-workers' conduct. What do you do when the supervisor's wife is the Human Resource Manager? Who do you communicate your grievances to when the supervisor's wife has the power to fire you and cover up the sexual advances? You go straight to the owner of the company.

Good business practice is not to make your wife the Human Resource Manager; that will eventually appear as a Conflict of Interest. When I think of the words harassment/discrimination, all of theses words come to mind: unwelcome, grievance, unreasonable, hostile, offensive, and intimidating work environment.

When I think of the word plot, words like conspiracy, demise, destruction, and wrong motive come to mind. Then I think about the purpose—who is doing the plotting? All of these questions are important to help the individual make a wise determination when evaluating whether or not you are being harassed or discriminated against.

Name names of each person, those in authority or those who are not in authority. Write everything in good faith, because the truth will out-live a lie. Corporate America is not going to play fair but do like I did, don't focus on the plot, focus on the plan. Don't focus on the cross; focus on the crown. The plot will thicken, but stay focused on the plan.

There is an old cliché that says "What you don't know won't hurt you." Well, I am here to tell you that Hosea 4: says, "My people are destroyed for the lack of knowledge!" We don't even know we are destroyed. To every reader, I believe the most important part of this book is to learn to Navigate through Corporate America. Let's face it, a man who can't work is a man who can't eat!

Navigation will help you pick up on codes and maneuver through trickery and deceptive tactics. Discerning of Spirit has also a benefit to Navigation. Discerning of Spirit helps you to recognize evasive and deceptive information from authority figures. Whatever they do or don't do, say or don't say, you will always be able to bring out results in your favor. When their plots are exposed, they recognize that we are smarter than they thought we were. Don't you dare believe they don't recognize your intelligence because whatever is in you can only stay hidden for a while? Some things are formed against you within the company to stop anyone in upper management from recognizing your talent. Remember this, "No weapon they form against you will prosper."

They had plans to write me up on March 12, 2001, which was a Monday. This write-up would have been the procedure for dismissal. I would have lacked 2 months in order for the employer to match my 401K benefits. I would have been fired unable to receive the SSI that would support me until I was awarded my settlement. I would not have written this book and learned the skills to expose such organized crime in Corporate America if I had not experienced these things first hand. Most of all, I would have missed the opportunity to see God bring me out with His mighty right hand.

I had this poster made and hung on the wall at each desk that was assigned to me that stated: *"My Present Position is Not an Indication of My Future Potential."* I was a file clerk then and now I am an author! I said, "My present position is not an indication of my future potential, my present position is not an indication of my future potential. I repeated this over and over again to myself and moved forward and learned to encourage myself!

Corporate America: They Had A Plot But God Had A Plan
Betty's Bits: Learn to encourage yourself!

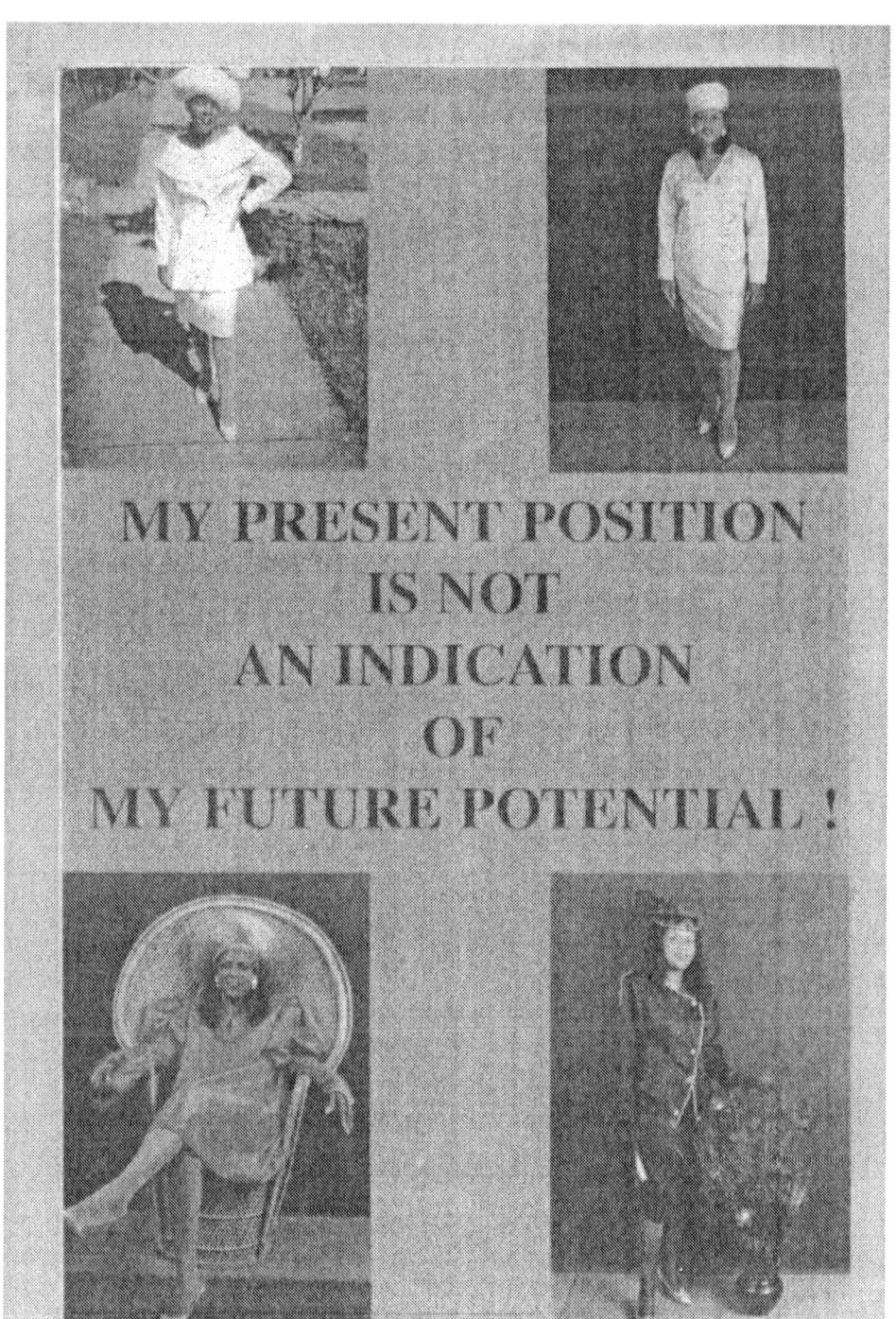

Place Your Vision Statement Before You

When I placed this poster up on the wall, my co-workers were only interested in the four designs I had made. But there was a VIP who read it and went and shared it with the other VIPs. Each one that came near my desk would search for the Vision Statement and one of them said to me, "I like that." I said, "I'm glad you do."

At that time I was in the position of a File Clerk and that was considered the lowest position in this office. I placed this vision statement in my face to keep me focused that I was in a pit but I was headed to a palace. While I was traveling through all of the obstacles I had to remember that no one could stop me but me. Stay focused and keep moving, there are many lonely days, many misunderstood ways, roller coaster emotions that seems to never stop, but ride it out, knowing that all things are working together for your good because you love the Lord. Remember, you are headed somewhere.

Chapter 13

NAVIGATING UP THE CORPORATE LADDER

Spiritual discernment is the navigator for the believer. When I first came to this job, a Hispanic lady said to me that I looked very young, even though she had heard that I had a 25-year-old son. My response to her observation was, "The Lord restores my Youth." This lady was a believer, and she looked at me so sincerely and said, "Maybe God has sent you here to be a light for this company." I can hear God. These words she said to me had God's signature written all over them.

She began to describe the employees to me; her description was horrible. This scripture from Psalms came to the forefront of my mind, "I would have fainted unless I had believed to see the goodness of the Lord in the land of the living." I became very observant and very watchful. I saw those in authority come together and maneuver and get co-workers written-up, and even fired. There was jealousy, retaliation, and petty attacks by one co-worker to another.

A wise man named Paul gave us valuable insight that we should keep at the forefront of our minds. "For we wrestle not against flesh and blood, but against rulers of darkness, rulers of this world, against spiritual wickedness in high places." Knowing the right time and knowing who your real enemy is, alerts us to when we are to schedule our promotions through Navigation. Promotion does not come from the north, east, south, or west; promotion comes from the Lord. There are destructive times in scheduling promotions. Low productivity is not the time to navigate. Budget cuts is not the time to navigate a schedule for promotion. We are missiles in flight, and we need to know when to travel, how to travel, and most of all, know when to change flight. Maybe you need to enroll in a class or prepare to transfer into another department in the company. Change could be your way to navigate away from toxic and difficult people, unreasonable managers, and supervisors with high estrogen levels. Certain flights take

Corporate America: They Had A Plot But God Had A Plan

you straight through and, depending on where you are going, you might have to take 2 or 3 flights to arrive on time. Some of us have prepared to fly, and we know how high to fly. Just as the enemy pilot has learned to fly their planes so low undetected under radar, Corporate America has learned to fly discrimination under the radar of the law and it flies strategically undetected by the law. Your attitude will determine your altitude, you need to be patient to see if this is really discrimination, and once you are very sure you are being discriminated against choose your best time to fly. Choose the best avenue to travel, and choose a department if you decide to stay with this company that best fulfills your goals and skills. I am arriving at the Kingdom of God at my designated time and I am right on schedule. For I believe I was sent to the Kingdom for such a time as this.

Betty's Bits: You need keen knowledge in navigating through the minefields, contrary forces, and dangerous waters in the workplace. These undercurrents flow in the form of fear that is designed to stop you from going to your next level. Beware of what I call **Folly Friday**. This is when a contrary force somehow blows near clock out time and stirs a negative forecast for the weekend and send you in a whirlwind. These forces have you worried about what's going to happen to you on Monday. Be on the Look Out!

Chapter 14

DISCERNING THE ATMOSPHERE

Remember, all truth is parallel. What does the forecast say today? To the man or woman that has learned how to listen to that inner voice, he or she will know how to prepare himself or herself. The forecast may be hostile, stressful deadlines or just a good day. Just as you prepare for the weather in, preparing for a hostile day can be just as important. If discrimination or some other negative force is manifesting in the natural world, it was given birth in the spiritual realm. The reason this is not clear enough to us is because the enemy knows how to throw a rock and hide its hand. It is sometimes hard to articulate discrimination because it is so dressed up—or should I say covered up—under unfairness and office politics. Discrimination can be dressed

Corporate America: They Had A Plot But God Had A Plan

up as unfairness if you cannot properly articulate it to your co-workers, they soon become annoyed and your peers view you as paranoid. Discerning the atmosphere will always introduce you to a defining moment. Defining moments give you a sense of purpose. These are moments marked out precisely, where there are no limitations and no boundaries. You are able to see clearly after the storms of life have tossed you to and fro.

This is a very popular song entitled: "I believe I can fly, I believe I can touch the sky." Discerning of Spirit is the atmosphere that believers fly in. Discerning of Spirit is the tool Christians use to navigate in a spiritual atmosphere like this.

Sometimes God sends people in our life to help navigate us to a destination that he has ordained. There are two types of winds that we encounter while flying. Everyone who plans to travel should be aware of turbulent winds and tailwinds. While traveling on the plane the turbulent winds will cause things to go up and down, and the tailwinds can cause us to get to our destination ahead of schedule. While traveling we must learn to trust the Navigator (Holy Spirit). The Navigator can see what we cannot see and hear what we cannot hear. I learned to weather adversity by trusting the Navigator.

Frederick Douglas said, "Blacks should keep their demands before the public. Booker T. Washington said that we should focus on economic gain. But in Corporate America, learning to maneuver, learning to navigate is essential to keeping your job during whirlwinds of manipulation. There are different atmospheres of tension that are expressed in the corporate world. All minorities have cultural differences but this should not be a reason for harassment or discrimination. Just because individuals are different that is no reason to disrespect them. I remember reading a story about a chicken in a hen house. This one chicken was different because he had a black spot on his head. The other chickens pecked at the black spot until he died, simply because he was different. That is the way harassment and discrimination maneuver and navigate in Corporate America. Because individuals are different, those toxic and difficult people peck on the spot of others' different personalities with petty, degrading, isolating, humiliating, remarks until they kill the character, the integrity of their fellow co-workers. Unfair treatment is not a crime, because life is not fair. But Corporate America has learned how to skillfully cross the boundaries from unfair treatment to harassment and discrimination. Cultural differences should be

Corporate America: They Had A Plot But God Had A Plan
expected because we are different in many ways. Even people of the same race still possess individual characteristics that make us who we are. However, we all are created equal.

Discerning Atmospheres Solutions for/In

Hostile Atmosphere
1. *Sit still.*
2. *Take a break (a must). Leave your work area.*
3. *Stay out of the battle zone area.*
4. *Go sit in your car and listen to a good tape/read the newspaper or a good book.*
5. *Go to lunch with a dear friend or family member who will encourage you.*

Stressful Atmosphere
1. *Take each break (a must). Leave your work area.*
2. *Call a good friend on break on your cell phone.*
3. *Meet a good friend for lunch.*
4. *Relax.*

Deadline Atmosphere
1. *Extreme tension, be a self-motivator.*
2. *Assure yourself that you will meet the deadline.*

3. *Map it out in your mind, prioritize and allow yourself time.*

4. *Delegate all tasks that do not require your expertise.*

5. *Again, take each break. Leave your desk.*

A Good Day Atmosphere

1. *Control your atmosphere.*

2. *Be a thermostat not a thermometer.*

    A. *Thermostat - controls/sets the atmosphere.*

    B. *Thermometer - adjust to atmosphere.*

Chapter 15

A PLOT VS. A PLAN

Corporate America cannot be brought to Justice for treating employees unfairly, but they can be exposed when unfair crosses the line to harassment and discrimination. They did not discriminate against me because I was black; they discriminated against me because I was not white. This was a 7-year lesson that cost me much pain and suffering. I observed Corporate America 40-48 hours a week. I could hardly wait to quit and go do something else in my field. But, God had destined me to go through these many experiences and also confirm these things I saw and discerned with my own heart and mind. God gave me peace in the midst of the storms: this is an overwhelming experience, where you're degraded, humiliated and isolated for 7 years. It produced traumatic stress that would have *denounced* me if it had not been for the Lord on my side. This experience left me feeling violated by a rapist. As long as I was silent, I was protecting my violators. I felt burned and as long as I covered up what Corporate America was allowed to do to me, this burn would not begin to heal. I had to air it out. Airing a wound helps it to heal quicker and properly, by putting a bandage on a burn will cause it not to heal, and forgiveness is the first step. The question that led me to this chapter in this book was, why and how did others stay in this type of abuse in Corporate America for so long?

Well, I thought it was for a paycheck, some might say it was for the mortgage, or for the luxury car, or for the children's education. Well, I believe it is because we are too weak to get out of it, yet, strong enough to stand up and take it. It is the fear of the unknown that causes people to stay in unhealthy situations. "The devil you know is better than the devil you don't know." God Forbid!

Harassment is a little sharper when it's revealed it cuts like a razor. Whenever there is a razor cut, most of the times you don't realize that you are cut until you see the blood. Now that can stand to be preached! This spirit of harassment comes from co-workers and those in authority, picking at you constantly, and if you engage back with this they would say you are too sensitive. This is how to recognize harassment, it is unsolicited, uncalled for, and unwarranted; therefore that makes it unlawful. Most of the time harassment concerns pettiness; that's the reason it is so hard to address because if you address it you somehow become as petty as the person/people that's harassing you. Harassment stems from jealousy and insecurity and most of all fear. F-E-A-R: False Evidence Appearing Real is the definition my friend gave me and I realized I had nothing to fear but fear itself.

In the movie "The Boycott," Barnard Rustin is sent to help Martin L. King take the boycott to the next level by ending Segregation in the South. The Boycott's attorney informs all the board members that there is a warrant for their arrest. They were afraid because these members were of the elite group—as teachers, lawyers, preachers, etc. However, since Barnard Rustin had crossed this bridge when he took a stand for his convictions a few years earlier, he caused them see the jailhouse for what it really was—a building. Most of all, they were not being arrested for doing anything wrong, they were being arrested for taking a greater stand for what was right. So they all went to the jailhouse and turned themselves in and this stand took the thunder out of the City Council's plot, and placed a lightning flash in the Boycott's plan. Barnard Rustin made them see the Big Picture. The Boycott went from Montgomery to the Nation.

Discrimination, for the most part, white America has not felt the brunt of discrimination like black America has. Jim Crows revealed most of the SIGNS that were visible in the 1930's through the 1950's. I said earlier how the counterfeiter learns how to update his currency. Corporate America has learned how to update discrimination: Sure we don't see "No Coloreds Eat Here," or "Whites Only" signs over the water fountain, "No Blacks Allowed!" in the window of restaurants. Nor do we see the signs that say, "If a white person needs a seat and there are none, a black person must release his." When a black person is asked to train a white person for a position in a company that a black person is qualified for and has performed competently, Corporate America is saying, "Give up your seat." When only white employees get to enjoy all the fringe benefits of the company, such as the company's suite, the company's cabin, or the company's travel privileges, Corporate America is saying "No Blacks Allowed."

Corporate America: They Had A Plot But God Had A Plan

When we are not allowed to drink from the fountain of higher pay and eat at the same economic tables in this land flowing with milk and honey, "What are you saying? "For Whites Only." Even though the SIGNS are no longer visible in 2004. Unfortunately, the "SIGNS" are still there! Yes, discrimination is still up and running.

I know there are some who do not agree and you are entitled to your opinion; however, Jesus said, "The poor we will have with us always, and whensoever ye will ye may do them good." My good to the poor is to make them knowledgeable so they will know how to arm themselves for this battle. Remember, this battle is not yours it's the Lord's!

Betty's Bits: Never <u>take</u> for granted the power of the CUSTODIAL DEPARTMENT. Most employees under estimate and over looked the CUSTODIAL department in Corporate America. Employees need to take a second look. What other person (s) while being invisible or perhaps one might say unseen has the privilege of going everywhere, and they are privy as to the inner working of any organization. During the day department heads are holding conversation as <u>if no one else</u> is in the room. After business hours they also have access to the same offices sans executives. While they are tenaciously working in a classroom, cafeteria, coutroom, conference room, CEO office, or the basement. Basement? Yes! After all where do all the discarded documents end up? Everyone talks in front of them about every thing and everybody, which gives them knowledge about everything. Knowledge is power. Don't ignore an employee who has the ear of the CEO's or the Custodial Department! As for the personal secretary and her relation with the CEO she may not be able to help you but she certainly can hurt you.

ALL MEN

The Constitution of the United States: "We have inalienable rights given to us by our Creator. ALL MEN ARE CREATED EQUAL, and have the right to life, liberty and the pursuit of happiness. We all want the same things. The things we all want place us on common ground. These things are not racial concerns these are human concerns. I believe as we focus on our similarities, rather than our differences, discrimination will no longer separate us; we can use it to UNITE us.

This amendment was put into place while these men were slave owners; this document placed these men in direct violation of the constitution they were writing.

We, as human beings want:

1. Health and strength
2. Children who will be successful and happy
3. Financial security

When we learn to embrace, accept and respect our differences we will appreciate our similarities. The same things that bother you bother me. The same things you want I believe everyone wants. Theses are not racial concerns these

Corporate America: They Had A Plot But God Had A Plan
are humanity concerns. The tools and techniques to liberate cultural diversities is to focus on our similarities rather than our differences. We all want the American Dream, and eat the American pie. "We not me." Likeness!

Betty's Bits: Inalienable rights are not capable of being given up or taken away. I have pain as my point of reference to the problems, read carefully and I believe my potential-power to overcome will point you to the solutions.

Chapter 16

WHAT QUALIFIES ME

I can't lead where I won't go and I can't teach what I don't know. I took CPR classes two years straight so I could learn all I needed to know to help support people in times of distress. I believe since I took this precise training, repeatedly, I am now qualified to do CPR to the body of Christ. I believe that these books that I have written will offer much support to individuals who are, going through what I have gone through. They need mouth-to-mouth resuscitation to put their hearts and mind in perspective after what they have experienced in Corporate America.

You saw what you saw; and they did what they did; now you tell what you know. St. John says, "Speak that you know and testify to that you have seen." Healing is the ultimate goal, so that we can get up and continue to run this race that is set before us. These books will help us to lay aside the weight of fear, the weight of stress, the weight of hopelessness. If you get back in the race and continue to run, you will win. I know because I won.

No one goes into Corporate America expecting this kind of treatment. A man or woman sacrifices their finances, their time and goes to school, goes to training to go into the work force to make a living and become successful. But instead they encounter such violations that it make you feel as though you are under terrorist attack.

No job is supposed to be like this. If I wanted to battle I would have enlisted in the Armed Forces. But, because I did enlist in the army of the Lord in 1962, I have gone through AIT. I have gone through Navy Seal. After 40 years of service I have earned the title of a veteran. I am being qualified to judge. Bishop Noel Jones always has us repeat, "I am a Gift to Somebody."

Will the right company claim your gift, will the right ministry claim your gift, will the right_____claim your gift? (You fill in the blank).

We all have been walked on at one time or another. However, from this day forward see yourself as a bridge for someone to cross over to the other side. I believe I told the story about the bridges we crossed in Arkansas. Some bridges could only hold a certain amount of weight, while some could hold quite a bit of weight. Look at a bridge from this point of view. Some people can't keep anything confidential, while some can. Know which bridge you have decided to use to help you make a successful transition. A bridge should be designed to connect you to the other side. Remember when your heart is guarded it is easier to allow the issues of life to flow. Faint hearts will affect every issue in your life and so will a wounded spirit. Well, think about the bridge you choose, connect yourself to both sides of an issue. I know how to abase and I know how to abound; I know in whatsoever state I am in to be content. (Wait quietly.) Oh yes, I am uniquely qualified to help.

These experiences that I have gone through and overcome have equipped me to be the author of this book, and qualified me to help others. My goal in writing this book is to help us as a nation to return to God's purpose and origination to stop the myths of man's interpretations. Because of violations of what

Corporate America: They Had A Plot But God Had A Plan
tradition has deemed us as black America to be, once we stepped out of the traditional box stigma blacks then we're viewed by white America as racist.

Chapter 17

CORPORATE CONSPIRACY

When the Holy Spirit is revealing to you the intention in the hearts of people, listen attentively, he may not repeat it. After he reveals this to you it is best to keep whatever he reveals to yourself. Because if you are constantly trying to explain it, to people who can't see, this tends to make people think of you as paranoid. Once you are labeled as paranoid, this makes your word less credible. Moreover, if you can learn to hold your peace, what is done in the dark will come to the light. Discrimination will reveal itself in the heat of the battle and will point to the person who manipulated the whole thing, whether publicly or privately.

Corporate conspiracy is real and running at an overwhelming speed. However, I know a revealer who is like a mighty rushing wind.

Silent conspiracy - The 2001 Presidential election was the highest form of Corporate Conspiracy and this silent conspiracy was exposed to the world. I informed the ballot people that the Democratic ballot sheet was different than our ballot sheet. After I informed the ladies at the polls that the papers that I had were not in line with the Ballot, I thought they would inform other voters of this, but they did not say a word about this error. I voted in the November 2000 election for a President. The poll I went to was full of the voters making mistakes, punching the wrong names, but the poll attendant said that Maxine Waters had announced on the radio that the ballot sheet was not in line with the poll voting ballot. But, I had not heard this announcement and I said to myself, how many other voters who were there did not hear the announcement on the radio? This Corporate Conspiracy caused us to select not elect our President.

Public reprimands are used in Corporate America as a form of discrimination, because once employees see you openly reprimanded by a manager, this isolates you from other employees, which keeps you without any support. This causes other employees to overstep their boundaries by saying and doing things they would not otherwise have done. Once it is public knowledge in Corporate America that they have a problem with an employee, the silent conspiracy, the unspoken request, goes into effect. Just because you carry a title that doesn't gain you respect. Respect is earned, not given. When an employee is respected more than the managers, this is not acceptable. When the only reason a manager is given respect is because of the title, there is a struggle with the employee who has gained the respect of co-workers, and a greater struggle when others in authority respect you. As the VIPs or managers and co-workers receive more respect from employees than the manager, then the struggle is on with that person the manager feels threatened by. When the vendors, new managers, come to your desk more than your managers' desk, get ready, the warfare is between you and that manger who is threatened by you. He will begin to operate in these three devices: Unspoken Request, Delegated Authority, and Body language. Body language is a powerful tool, used negatively or positively. Example: when a woman is interested

Corporate America: They Had A Plot But God Had A Plan

in a man she can let him know without saying a word by using her body language.

Individuals who have been with the company at least 7 years mostly use the Code of Delegated Authority covers. This person used to implement the plot is someone who is familiar with corporate games carries this out. If all of a sudden this employee begins to operate with more authority, someone of higher authority has given them the power to do so. Delegated Authority has to be handed down from an upper degree of management because it has to be cleared by someone who knows the policies well. Then once a manager gives this report to the Higher Authority and he reacts to the employee in a derogatory way, it can be perceived as discrimination and harassment. Once you have been singled out for their witch-hunt, those in authority form an alliance to carry out their plot.

People surrounding me and people involved in fulfilling God's purpose, would always reassure me. I crossed boundaries that people around me would not. Whenever a person has the courage to blaze a trail, don't add to the problem, but add to the solution. If you are afraid to take the stand with them, pray for the person and God will give that person favor. This person has been sent to make the job atmosphere better for all those concerned. I stepped across the lines of my own limitations, but what they could not understand was that God had delegated my authority. And the liberty I walked in was only because of God. He called me unto His Purpose. When God has delegated you, you say things that others can't say and you do things that others can't do.

Well, after studying the managers in my situation, I saw them become very intimidated. They were very uncomfortable, and avoided saying and doing certain things around me. But after they had received authority from someone higher than themselves, I saw Mickey Mouse around 9:00 a.m. turn into Mighty Mouse around 2:00 p.m. Under normal circumstances, I would not speak up for myself. But after I found out that the God I served is truly real, I had a boldness that wouldn't let me hold my peace. Boldness comes when God delegates the authority.

Betty's Bits*:* Delegated authority I considered it as natural, ordinary and normal. This could appear supernatural, extraordinary and abnormal when those in authority see you walk in it so easily without any signs of intimidation. How intimidating?

Beyond Faith—Trust

We have all heard this before, "For we are to walk by faith and not by sight." What do you do when everything around you has failed? You go beyond faith to trust. "Trust in the Lord with all thine heart and lean not to your own understanding but in all thy ways acknowledge Him and He will direct thy path." That is certainly beyond faith.

Trust Him to turn everything around to your good. This is easier said than done, when you see your marriage failing, and when you see the children not functioning because the marriage is failing, when you see you have now been without work for over a year, and the savings account is now exhausted, when you see the gas tank linger on 3 gallons, and you don't have bus fare for Rapid Transit District. It's easier said than done when you see things not coming to pass although you know God spoke to you, showed you, and revealed to you the very opposite way of what is happening, when you see those around you that have in their power to help you, close the heart of compassion, when you see the time when you can't kill anything and won't let anything die. When you see your own heart about to faint and a spirit of heaviness weigh on your brow, when you see those that were for you are slowly turning against you because this now requires them to leave their comfort zones and testify that what you have said is true. When you see that people's jobs are on the line because it is stated in the EEOC charges that if any employee is retaliated against for testifying on the behalf of the employee who was violated, that employee will have the right to sue. When you see them pull a loophole out of the judicial box to substantiate their response to your allegations, after having been voted employee of the month, after having several witnesses present evidence to backup your charges, after having three doctors confirm what you have said is true, and then you are told, "Through all of this evidence we cannot prove that this is discrimination." You better step up a notch from beyond faith to trust. Because this is not based on what anyone can see, this is based on what you know. If God is for you He is more than the whole world against you. T-R-U-S-T. I'm reminded of the Lakers about 2 or 3 years ago when the Lakers were behind and it seemed as though there was no way that they could win that game. The commentators had counted them out, their fans had counted them out, and even some of their team members had counted themselves out. The team put their heads together and made enough points to tie the score. This

Corporate America: They Had A Plot But God Had A Plan
caused the Lakers and the Blazers to go into overtime. When they went into overtime the Blazers, having to push their skills to that next level under NBA pressure, fell apart. However, Shaq had already learned to perform under NBA pressure.

Well the Lord said to me, "Betty, you are going into overtime because the score is tied, but remember, I brought you through faith through a challenging marriage, I brought you through faith through the floods of sickness, and you know me now as a healer." I learned during overtime in my marriage, my healing, and my finances, that without faith it was impossible to please Him. "He said, "Remember, I brought you in faith. When you did not see Me, when you could not trace My hand, you learned to trust My heart."

Betty's Bits: I would like to dedicate this chapter to my friend for her words of encouragement at my defining moment. She said that I had to go beyond faith to trust. She said, "Betty, write this chapter and dedicate this one to me." My friend, I pray that you are pleased with my interpretation of beyond faith to trust. My friend strengthened me to go through, to see what the end would be. This was an even greater act of Trust because God had already permitted me to write the final chapter on a verdict that I had not received. Now faith is the substance of things hoped for the evidence of things not seen!

Betty Marie Knight

The 23rd Psalms for the Workplace

Unknown Author

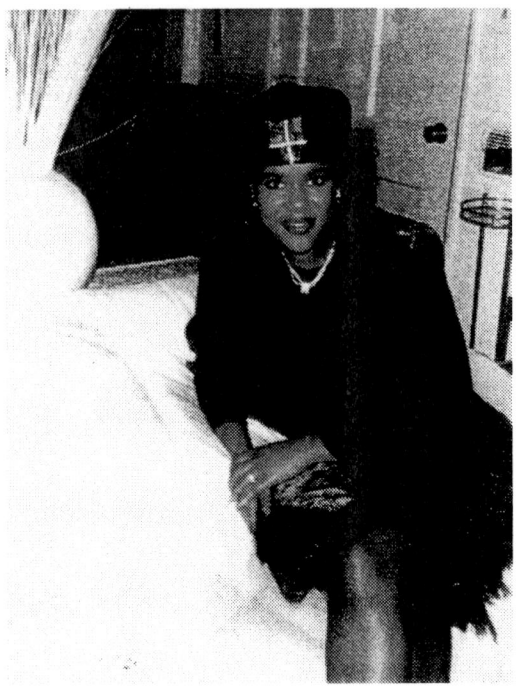

The Lord is my boss, and I shall not want.

He gives me peace, when chaos is all around me.

He reminds me to pray, before I speak in Anger.

He restores my sanity,

He guides my decisions that I might honor Him in all I do.

Even though I face absurd amounts of e-mail,

Corporate America: They Had A Plot But God Had A Plan

System failures, copier jams, back ordered supplies,

unrealistic deadlines,

Staff shortages, budget cutbacks, red

tape, downsizing, gossiping co-workers

and whining customers, I won't give up, for You are with me.

Your presence, peace and power will see me through.

You raised me as your own, even when the company threatens

to let me go.

Your loyalty and love are better than a bonus check.

Your retirement plan beats any 401K, and when it's all said

and done,

I'll be working for you a whole lot longer!

Thanks be to God!

Betty Marie Knight

Chapter 18

TERMINATION VS. DISCRIMINATION

Termination focuses on the plot, and the plot is concerned with the conspiracy, the limitations, and the end. However, determination focuses on the plan. The plan concerns souls being saved, resolution, and destiny. The plan is courageous. After what I experienced I moved with true determination that would drive me to expose the devil and help others to overcome.

In Corporate America, once the decision has been sent down and individuals are fired, such an uneasy feeling begins to fill the room that it is almost unbearable.

I watched a lot of people, both men and women, get fired. The management huddles together, discussing how they are going to pull this off and humiliate the employee as much as possible.

Betty Marie Knight

I watched managers walk in and out of personnel. I watched personnel managers go to the check printer in a suspicious kind of way, trying to keep everyone from seeing whose name is on the check being issued. Payday is not for another two weeks. The atmosphere is so tense. All day long everyone sits wondering, is it me? Until it is time to clock out, the employee is called into the manager's office. Sometimes the manager who is the prime supporter of the termination leaves early, leaving the personnel managers to do his dirty work. Now don't get me wrong here, if an employee is not performing her job duties, then that employee is not a team player. When the employee sows discord in the office, I agree, termination is warranted. But, to terminate an employee because of the pettiness of other women, because a woman is attractive, because a woman dresses well, because a woman is gifted, because a woman has favor, because a woman has wisdom, because the individual threatens management, is not a reason for termination of any employee. When managers harass an employee because her estrogen level is up or down, this is extremely unfair.

Now the turnover costs at this company were well over $1,000,000 a year—for hiring and training new employees, drug testing and physical examinations. I learned that Corporate America is so crafty that when your reason for termination is written-up, it is written in such a way as to stop all employees from receiving unemployment benefits until they are able to receive employment elsewhere. In my case of receiving a check from EDD, this company had not approved my unemployment benefits. After all of their civil rights violations, to add insult to injury, they said No! I began my next fight, the same way you as an employee would—not wanting reveal or compromise the position that they placed you into while being employed. So I stated my reasons as to why I took a leave of absence and after I told my side of the story then my benefits were approved. In Unemployment Benefits Appeals, you can use witnesses also. Use what you got, and all you got. Like they say in Corporate America, push the envelope. Whatever you do, please do not allow Corporate America to place you in a compromising position. The compromise can be the determining factor as to your being allowed to stay or go. For sure, you will eventually be discharged. The reason for your discharge will be made known to you when you find out that you did not qualify for unemployment benefits. Now for the unemployment benefits there is a new law added, Catch 22: I asked people in several different "One Stops," "Cal jobs," and "EDD" what is their best explanation of it and I repeat, "You are ____ if you do and you are _____ if you don't!" Need I say more?

Unemployment benefits can ease the load and help ends meet until employment is re-established with another company or you become the CEO of your own company. Listen to me, mentally and emotionally we are not strong enough to handle Corporate America's shortcomings any longer. People are destroyed for a lack of knowledge.

If I had not gone out on stress I would not have received these skills. When I was placed under stress leave, I was ignorant of all of the things we have rights to. Civil Rights stop Corporate America from treating people worse than animals. As a matter of fact, the people I worked with treated their dogs and cats better than they treated me. So, being released from work under stress was a blessing in disguise. I thought I was a strong, intelligent, black woman. Abuse has a way of keeping a person tied to it; a person is somehow too weak to leave, but strong enough to stay.

Corporate America: They Had A Plot But God Had A Plan

In Corporate America, strong black men are viewed as a threat. What Corporate America does is put black men in positions where they are forced to stand up for themselves. Once they stand up for themselves, "for their legal rights," Civil Rights, are then labeled as a disgruntled employee or a troublemaker. Strong black men will be fired or put into low management roles so they can be controlled. This is also used to sow discord between races for Corporate America's purposes. I'm not disgruntled; however, I am determined. There is a difference.

Betty's Bits: Unfair treatment is called grievance. The law doesn't have federal statutes to protect labor laws unfair. But as discrimination—Federal Civil Rights protects us.

Chapter 19

STRESS OR TEST

Cross Over

On August 30, 2001 I sat up in my bed to write these books to expose to the world my experience, the unlawful practice, exercised in Corporate America. I don't believe this was done to me because I was black, I believe this was done to me because I wasn't white. After only sleeping 2-3 hours a night for 2 1/2 years, after suffering from multiple

bilateral breast cysts, after experiencing chest pains, after eating 300 mg of Zantac all day long, after headaches, after hurting so bad that I wanted to die, after being humiliated and still walking in love, after being the brunt of jokes, after doing whatever I could to hold on to my faith, their attitude was business as usual. After

I filed my charge against the company it was stated that I was not under stress. I was afraid of being fired. Being fired was not the stress; the strain was being stretched beyond a proper limit, being injured by putting forth too much effort for a company that could not see my value.

I remained at the company for five years. Once I stepped on their grounds my gifts begin to flow in such maturity this woman in authority was intimidated by them.

Well, I worked with her and finished my assignment, and about two months before the assignment was over, it was estimated that I would stay on as a permanent employee.

So, excited, I went back home that day and prepared to go through intense training. I was being trained in the affairs of man, to prepare me for the intense training in the affairs of God, perfecting me to handle my walk through Corporate America.

To every reader of this book, I have shared with you things that I've gone through. If you keep these things abreast, these facts about Corporate America, they will no longer be able to get away with things like discrimination and harassment.

When you start a new job, or even if you've been on your job for twenty years, I suggest you begin a journal explicitly pertaining, to that job. And every time they write you up, they are preparing you for dismissal. This file is their journal to help substantiate their reasons for dismissing you. Remember, keep your dairy up-dated because their file on you will surely be kept up to date.

You have heard the old cliché that says, "Sticks and stones may break my bones but words can never hurt me." We all will agree that this is not true after what we have experienced in life. Your self-esteem takes a hit with resentment and jealousy; this will affect your heart. Distress and intense sorrow will affect your self-esteem. This can be a hostile atmosphere to work under especially when all of the negative energy and negative conditions are aimed at a single individual. When a fighter is hit below the belt he needs a time out count or call to get his wind back, and his opponent loses points for hitting below the belt. Well, when your self-esteem has taken a hit below the belt, this will affect your judgment and your judgment will affect your performance. This could be a breakthrough or a break down. Stress or a test to see if you can hold things together right through here, everything is going so crazy but you can do it. You are still that wonderful person, that strong confident person that can do whatever you set your heart and mind to do. There is an old proverb that says, "Guard your heart with all diligence for out it flows the issues of life." Issue - is a final conclusion or decision about something arrived at after consideration. Guard yourself from toxic people who are there to tear you down and not build you up. I repeat, "Guard your heart with all diligence for out of it flows the issues of life." Remember, a flatterer won't say to your face what he says behind your back." On the other hand, an encourager will say to your face what he says behind your back." Think about it. I see people as bridges, some bridges are to be walked over and others are to be ridden over, however some bridges are only built to hold a certain amount of weight. Some bridges can hold up to 500 lbs, and then there are some that can hold 500 tons. We need to be sure of which bridge is which when it is time to cross over. Don't place the weight of 500 tons on a bridge that is only designed to hold 500 lbs. This could be a matter of life or death. Please remember, this bears repeating, a bridge has to be able to touch both sides of an issue, in order to get you across successfully. I believe I'm qualified to touch both sides of the issue. I know what it's like to be abound and to abase, I have repeated this proverb several times because I want to drive

Betty Marie Knight

this point home to you. Proverbs says, to guard your heart with all diligence for out of it flows the issues of life. Guard your affections for they will influence everything else in your life. Use the right bridge and cross over!

Chapter 20

GO THROUGH MEDIATION

I think mediation is the best resolution method. I believe if this company had it to do all over they would have settled with me on June 20th, 2001 almost a year ago today. They never knew what hit them when God revealed what they never wanted anyone to know. On June 20th 2001, almost a year ago, all of my fears were gone and faith took her rightful place in my heart. All the VIPs and managers that attended the meeting knew that day that I had my day in court. I realized that day that they were all on neutral ground and I witnessed with my own eyes that outside of the company's property they all were just mere men and women like me, and their power was limited. I saw their lawyer was not as qualified as they had blown him up to be. So I drew strength that wherever this fight was about to take me I was ready for the journey, the fight, the battle, and I knew in my heart I could go the distance.

During mediation you have a right to have someone with you. You have a right to bring a person as a representative. Just inform the mediator the name of this person and the mediator will inform the company. Likewise the mediator will inform you as to who the company is bringing with them. Be on time because there will be so much tension. They don't really know how much you know and they are still going to play those games they played at the office, but remember you are not at the office. The office is their dominion and they are in charge; however, at the Federal State Building the Civil Rights law is in charge. View the fact sheets in this book so that you may understand the charges and can articulate them accurately. Corporate America is hoping that you cannot articulate the charges well enough to stand up in a court of law. May I testify about the EEOC investigator that crossed my path? She was a very strong woman, very stern, with a healthy level of confidence. She did not feel adequate enough to represent me so she seemed frustrated with me each time we talked. When I spoke with her I remembered

Corporate America: They Had A Plot But God Had A Plan

the movie Armistad–in this movie Djimond Hounson plays the slave Cinque, and his lawyer John Quincy Adams is played by Anthony Hopkins who is not qualified to represent Cinque and the other slaves in a court of law. However Cinque understood there were boundaries in the water but he did not know quite how to make it relevant in his case. There is a young man that Morgan Freeman helped Adams find, who spoke English and interpreted Cinque's native language. So the interpreter went to the lawyer, and would interpret in English exactly what Cinque's told him to say to his lawyer. After the 7th interpretation, the lawyer with the help of Cinque's insight, was able to adequately represent the slaves in a fair and just trial.

Well, that's what I experienced with my case at the EEOC. The investigator did not understand how to represent me, so I went to the office on April 5th, 2002 and used the KISS method (Keep it Simple Stupid) to share my hindsight and my insight with her. Then it became plain as to how she was to fight my case. Up until that time she had played the devil's advocate, until the Lord revealed to me that she did not understand my job so she could not articulate it well enough to give me a fair trial. So I interpreted it to her and she said to me at the end of this section that I made a wise decision to come in and have this conference instead of a phone conference because the phone conference had failed greatly and we were at wits end with one another.

With all of that in mind I would like to offer you an incentive, a bonus that can help you go through when you are ready to give up or let go. I can offer you that kind word, tools of knowledge for your loyalty, for your commitment, for your hard work in Corporate America, these two simple words "Good Job and Well Done," Now take all these tools and win your case.

Though the EEOC mediation is designed as a resolution to stop court if both parties agree, all my fears became faith if and when I would have my day in court, and that's what mediation does; it gives you a preview of coming attractions of your day in court. The date is set after you go to the EEOC and file a charge. Then the EEOC investigator explains to you how this procedure works. Use the KISS method so that you can articulate accurately and cause the lawyers and the human resource managers to go back with the report that they are going to have to rewrite or add a chapter to the Employee Handbook. Statistics concerning discrimination in Corporate America are still at an all time high as of May 2002. Statistic states that 70% of most illnesses are caused by stress. Think back after you were unlawfully terminated, how they stopped your unemployment. This check could have helped your family make ends meet until your next employment. Think back how managers are encouraged to betray employees. Think back as to how you were used as the "scapegoat" because management failed to check the financial report and catch that $23,000 dollar loss and that $5,000 penalty for not meeting the deadline. Why do so many discrimination cases go unsolved? Why are so many discrimination cases not filed? Why is there still discrimination? Because most people don't believe that discrimination still exists. And the most important reason is that discrimination is hard to prove in a court of law, and it is twice as hard to articulate it so that it is viewed as an unlawful act.

Communication Skills

Tools and techniques that will help liberate us from discrimination. It's not what you say it's how you say it! People who are argumentative should be taught to use a gentle approach. Be slow to speak and quick to listen. Being a good listener will earn you rights to speak, proving the opening to share honed and empowering knowledge to impact the listener.

1. **Listen, then begin your comment with these words, "to add too what he or she has said …"**
2. **Listen, with courtesy while waiting on the other person to finish their comments, instead of with an attitude.**
3. **The old cliché says, "It's not what you say it's how you say it," true, however, tone, technique, thoughts, and selective words construct excellent communication skills.**

Communications skills are very important as well as very necessary when dealing with toxic managers and co-workers. I was asked this question from a toxic white female supervisor, "Why do your race get mad when we used the N word? You call each other that and you don't get mad?" My response, "When we as a black race use the N word, it is not defined as a race it is defined as a characteristic."

We all have terms we use within our race about our race that only that race can say and we feel it is politically correct. Such as, Hispanics call each other SAs, or wetbacks. Or the white race will call each other a peckerwood, or redneck. Italians, they use the

Corporate America: They Had A Plot But God Had A Plan

term wasp and not be offended. Just as "the-dozens," cannot be played outside a race or family concerning this matter, these terms can come under cultural diversities as well as communication skills. (KJV SLC)

We all have heard in our walk of life that knowledge is power. And in the Christian walk of life we do know that the TRUTH you know will make you free. Discrimination is another form of slavery. The steel chains that once binded our hands and feet, are still being used to bind our minds. How? I 'm glad you asked that question. When we allow Corporate America to define us. When we remain on a job that we are responsible for making into a Billion Dollar Corporation and that company will not pay you what you are worth, and at the same time slowly make you believe that you are incompetent in the position, this is a mental chain. **WHY?** We're born with unique communication skills. I heard a man of God say. As a Black race, we have had long distance service years and years before AT&T ever thought of it. Our ancestors would communicate on the drums to the others tribes miles and miles away, and this strong foundation of communication is still instilled in our race. Our ancestors used "coded song" during slavery to communicate with the other slaves and to keep the slave masters in the dark .

The true White forefathers of the Willie Lynch era are now dead and The Willie Lynch theory skipped a generation. These are the men and women that built their companies with integrity. However, their children, who this theory has been instilled into, these are now the CEO's of Corporate America. The younger master's (CEO's) present a new complicated problem. This is why Corporate America has the new name "Modern-Day Slavery." The **real** Question is WHY? Why is the Black race continually under attack, when we answer this question (WHY) the solution is simple. If we will not take the time to find out the PURPOSE of any thing, abuse and misuse is inevitable. **WHY?** Fraud is defined as deceit; trickery; cheating. Corporate fraud seems to be at the forefront of the media since 2000 due to *Enron*: The highest form fraudulence of practiced is Character Assassination in Corporate America. I give 150% of myself for better or for worse, and recognize I could think outside of the box and was capable of functioning while receiving pay raises, and employee of the month awards because of my outstanding performance. Because of their insecurities a plot was implemented to defame

Corporate America: They Had A Plot But God Had A Plan

my character. That is Corporate Fraud. I believe this is traumatic experience because we are taught at a very young age that doing a good job will be rewarded. Welcome to the real world.

Betty's Bits: God has given us five senses. Because of my senses and how knowledgeable I am in using them all for communication, I have an awareness that others seem not to have, and I have a strength that's not my own. Each one of these senses can be used for communication. We all think that our mouth is only for communication, however, the touch is a form of communication. Touch communication is when something is too cold or too hot. Seeing is a form of communication; sight will alert you while driving if you are going over the speed limit. Yes, hearing is a form of communication; just as an alarm will alert a blind person of a fire. Taste is a form of communication. Taste buds communicates whether something is sweet or if something is bitter. The Smell is an awesome form of communication, just "asks" the bloodhound!

Sexual Orientation

We all have a past; we all have done wrong things and come up short. When we gauge our past by the One True Ruler and measure ourselves according to His straight line, we all miss the mark. We all have something we have done that we pray that God will keep in the closet. So therefore we are all Closet "Homophobes".

Betty Marie Knight
Mail and Male/Fee Mail and Female

If our secrets were to get out, would we like them to determine how we are viewed now in society? What we have done may or may not be grounds for discrimination.

Even from a Biblical standpoint, discrimination is not the answer, the Creator hates the sin but He loves the sinner. Therefore, discrimination is not the tool nor technique which we should govern ourselves by. There is no discrimination in the word of God for the Bible says, *"Whosoever shall call on the name of the Lord shall be saved!"*

Betty's Bits: I am not careful as to how I will answer this matter; my convictions are on Biblical principles, however, I have learned not to dislike the person but to dislike the practice. Let the wheat and the tares grow together and He will separate! Sure we were all born in sin and shaped in iniquity. I know you feel that you were born that way, however you don't have to die that way.

Chapter 21

SABOTAGE CHARACTER

Who Sets The Tone?

In every walk of life those in charge have set the tone. In education, if a teacher is

displeased with a student, the other students will look at him and say things to him that will express the same disgust that they see their teacher show. This behavior will be repeated over and over by students from kindergarten thru college. Transferring of Spirits.

In the church, if the sheeps always see the shepherd rebuking or mishandling a sheep, the other members will also isolate, and mishandle this same member also. When the members see a shepherd disrespect his wife, this opens the door for others to disrespect her also.

On a farm I was once told a story about a chicken. If a chicken is different the other chickens will mistreat him. If that chicken is born with a black spot on his head the other chickens will peck the black spot until the chicken is dead, trying to remove the thing that makes him or her different. This is exactly the behavior that's repeatedly used on employees that are different.

I faced daily incidents with a co-worker making derogatory remarks. I had to turn the other cheek and realize that this spirit enjoyed insulting me every chance she got. So I made a decision that I was going to put a stop to this kind of behavior since management had not been able to put a stop to it. Whenever this co-worker was about to speak to me, I would say to another worker. "Listen to what she is about to say to me. She continued to speak this way to me after I had alerted others to listen. I knew then that I had to take a stand, a very bold stand, and use this co-worker as an example. I waited until she had said everything and then I told her, "If I told you what you reminded me of I would have you sitting there crying." I went on to say, "Let this be your last time making derogatory comments to me. My job

Corporate America: They Had A Plot But God Had A Plan
performance has never been an issue, you all are mad because of my looks." I felt it was time to expose this devil that continues to use my job performance, my hairstyles, my dress style, and my poetry gift, as a smokescreen to play the petty games that women play and do to one another, when this was really racism.

I walked into the ladies' room and I was so angry that tears came in my eyes. I told Sharon, one of the managers, that my mother had faced this same kind of cruelty from women all of her life. My mother would tell me over and over again the reason why these women attack you so much is because of the way you look which has so much to do with my race because of the many racial slurs that were made. I asked my manager why management could not stop these co-workers from saying these negative remarks to me, and Sharon said, "Betty, the reason why management can't control or stop these employees from doing and saying these derogatory things to you is because management has set the tone."

Dear America, when Christmas comes Again:

I was asked to be a speaker for a Family Conference hosted by Dr. Dione Washington, founder of Quantum Leap Ministries.

Betty Marie Knight
Well, as I was preparing to leave the library, I looked to my left and there was a book that caught my attention called. "Dear America, when Christmas comes Again." I opened the book up and began to read. When World War I was finally over, nearly ten million men had lost their lives on the battlefield as well as the destruction of it's building and landscape. The world was a different place says Beth Seidel Levine, in World War I Diary of Simmons Spencer. Twenty million were wounded. Due to the terrible battle injuries, the war also created a need for a new kind of medicine-physical reconstruction or rehabilitation. France & England already had reconstruction aide program in place. The Physical therapy profession was born. Because of the wounds and the terrible battle a new kind of medicine was birthed. Because of the warfare that I faced in Corporate America for over eight years left me in a traumatic state. This was so traumatic because we are taught at a very young age that when a job is well done you can be rewarded. Not in Corporate America. I pray that these truths and principles will create a new kind of medicine. Discrimination in the 1900's was verbal; in the 2000's it is visual. In the 1900's, the atmosphere was charged with hatred. In the 2000's the atmosphere is charged with hostility. I was able to prove it was the race card.

Corporate America: They Had A Plot But God Had A Plan

I was told if you pull the race card prove it, it is a pattern that's practice. Discrimination has a pattern. Discriminate Webster defines it as able to make or see fine distinctions; discerning. I believe new kind of medicine should focus on our similarities and rather than on our differences.

Betty's Bits: The people you surround yourself with must not be considered lightly. We tend to allow people to affirm and validate us who are really not qualified to do so. The people we choose might have a poor self-image or be insecure. Because of their insecurities they will sabotage your character by the negative and derogatory remarks they somehow continue to repeat. Time will reveal it all, be slow to speak and quick to listen.

Chapter 22

TRANSITION FROM HOME BACK TO WORK

Safeguards when returning back to work

I had been out on Post Traumatic Stress Disorder for a little over a year. My disability was exhausted and my doctor released me to return back to work. However, that was easier said than done. I needed transitional support because all of my fears returned. The EEOC doesn't offer a bridge to help you cross back into Corporate America unless you were unlawfully terminated. This is where my family, my friends, my manicurist, Jeffery, was a great help to me. I said, "Jeffery, I'm preparing to return back to work." So Jeffery said, "Go back with your best foot forward." He asked me if I wanted my nails cut down because that was one of the reasons they used to justify my write up. However, another guy did the same job I did and made the same identical mistakes, but his nails were never an issue. So I got Jeffery to cut my nails down very short. Then my stepmother from St. Louis called me to encourage me and to see how my first day was. My children began to say, "Mama don't fear God is with you." My friends called me for prayer and edified me with the word. Yes, I will admit this was easier said than done. My pastors prayed and asked God to confirm this move to me over and over again. I know if God is leading me by His Spirit.

On February 14th, 2001 I was so afraid about what they were going to do to me the next day at work, but I saw myself in a dream singing, "I'm holding on and I won't let go of my faith." The Spirit of the Lord said to me, "Give it to me! Give it to me all. Remember this night, I won't let you fall!" Well, I decided since He had brought me this far I might as well let Him take me all the way. All the way from home back into Corporate America, because He is my navigator and He had revealed to me that I could

trust Him to see what I could not see and hear what I could not hear. I will admit, not every one will have the favor that I had, but not everyone will have to face what I faced. I needed great grace and I had it.

There are three kinds of people: People that make things happen, people that watch things happen, and people who say what happened? I'm one of those people that make things happen. People that make things happen are people that know their God, and because they know their God they are capable of exploits. People who know their God are thermostats. And people who don't know Him are thermometers. Thermostats control the atmosphere; thermometers measure and adjust to the atmosphere. Go back to Corporate America and be a thermostat; control you atmosphere now that you know how to navigate in a strange land. Use all the support systems that you have. Call a hotline. Kaiser offers a support line. Your church offers support; other churches offer support; take advantage of them all. I draw strength from this when I realized that I had the power to make a decision for my life, you better know no man has that kind of power over your life! When those in authority over you want to place you in a box and keep you in their control; tell you what they think you should do no matter how unjustified it may be,

Corporate America: They Had A Plot But God Had A Plan

and use their opinion to validate your decision on whether you go or whether you stay.

Kunta Kinte ran away over and over again not because he was rebellious but because he had outgrown the box of slavery. So in the movie "Roots" he risked getting his foot cut off simply because Kunta just did not fit in this little arrangement anymore. This is that House N_____ Syndrome. To be a House N_____ to the white man, this was considered a luxury, and this was as far up in authority a black woman could climb. Stay in your place and do not step out of the box that we have put you in. I would not have chosen this path if I had power over my own life, and when those in authority place you in a corporate box and you won't fit into it, they will become threatened. Remember you are a thermostat not a thermometer.

Safeguards - the best safeguards in returning back to Corporate America is a witness! Can I get a witness?

Safeguards from retaliation. E-mail me and give me some suggestions.

Safeguards from discrimination. E-mail me and give me some suggestions

The Union is a safeguard, or should I say should be one.

Retaliation can come in many ways, that's even harder to prove. They have the power to say whether they feel you have the skills or qualifications be promoted to and/or to receive a pay raise.

What safeguards can be written to expose the practices of harassment/discrimination? What laws can be written into our Civil Rights Act that can help safeguard once an employee has reported discrimination.

Should an employee be violated for standing up for her or himself?

Feel free to write and give me some solutions to help stop this or at least expose it. Don't forget to write!

Corporate America: They Had A Plot But God Had A Plan

Betty's Bits: Corporate America is in need of a Champion. When it was time for Slavery to be abolished we needed a Champion. God sent Abraham Lincoln. When it was time for segregation to be rendered illegal, we needed a Champion. God sent Rosa Parks and Martin L. King. Now that it is time to bridge the gap, Corporate America needs a Champion. God is sending you and me.

Stay In Your Race

Run

In a race you have several kinds of runners.

Sprinters,

100-yard dash,

440 relays,

and 880 relays and marathon runners:

There are three things the Company is responsible for:

1.) Sponsors

2.) Supporters

3.) Donations

There are three things the Runners must do to qualify:

1.) Communicate

2.) Prepare

3.) Apply

I am reminded of the race that the Revlon Corporation sponsored. This three-mile walk-a-thon was held on the weekend of Mother's Day in the year of 2000. This effort was for the fight against breast cancer. We had only a few days to prepare for this because the one that was supposed to get everything in order dropped the ball. So I was then put in charge of helping to pull this off in time. As Runners we had to get T-shirts that had the company's name on them, and also get each person to fill out the

Corporate America: They Had A Plot But God Had A Plan

form that made the company that sponsored us accountable for the runners.

Here we are in a race; the company is the sponsor and the managers are the supporters. Twenty of the women in the business office volunteered to walk a total of three miles. We are the runners in this company and we have agreed to work eight hours a day for five days.

There were several departments:

    Sales Dept.

    Finance Dept.

    Service Dept.

    Personnel Dept.

The prizes are our bonus, incentive, promotion, and our paycheck. We are one Team; therefore if we are to run successfully we must remember, "This race is not given to the swift nor is the battle to the strong but to him that can endure until the end."

In order for this to be a successful day there must be:

    1.) Communication

    2.) Preparation

    3.) Application

Team players are to be efficient as possible; that's if the next department is to hand the baton to the next runner without being penalized. The paperwork must be handled correctly. Remember, a house divided against itself cannot stand.

Allow me to share this testimony with you so that you can understand why you should stay in your race! My company participated in the fight against breast cancer sponsored by Revlon. Since this was my first walk-a-thon, I disciplined and trained myself by going down to the alley and walking every weekend.

1.) I observed several things such as weights, which could so easily beset us as runners.

My business manager and my office manager both were new grandmothers, and they both decided that they wanted the Grandmother of the Year Award for this Mother's Day.

So they both asked their daughters to bring their new granddaughters to the walk-a-thon so that they could push them in the strollers.

2.) Another co-worker loved magazines. The Revlon Corporation gave away 15 of the most popular magazines. This particular co-worker did not believe that her magazines would be there when she returned so she carried all fifteen magazines while running this race.

3.) I observed other co-workers who could have ran this race much quicker, however, they had peers who could not keep up with their pace and this made them reluctant to finish before them. They felt if they finished first they would receive some form of retaliation. One of their peers/runners was a supervisor. After observing the weights, I came to this conclusion; we are all on a mission, and once we agree to run the race, stay in the race.

Stay in the race, run it at your pace, with your best face. If you make a mistake remember Grace! Here you are today lining up for an 8-hour run. Listen, I repeat, my managers are campaigning for the Grandmother of The Year Award, by pushing their granddaughters in strollers. This was not wrong, however, it was definitely a weight.

Secondly, as for my co-worker who loved magazines and carried all fifteen magazines on a 3-mile race—this was not wrong; however this was definitely weight.

Thirdly, co-workers who were reluctant to finish the race before peers in order to avoid retaliation from supervisors and

Betty Marie Knight

co-workers—was certainly not a sin, however, this was definitely a weight.

Today I stand as forerunner. I was placed in this race many years ago. I ran through segregation, I ran through isolation, I ran through frustration, I ran through racial discrimination. Therefore, I'm still standing because I stayed in my race.

This Race has nothing to do with the color of your Skin but the Content of your Character.

Chapter 23

A LESSON FROM A FROG

Life is filled with swift transitions, none on earth who can stand. Build your hope on things eternal, hold to God's unchanging hand. Life is full of lessons, some we will repeat and some we will learn and move forward. Everything changes—life, friends, hopes, careers, ages, times, and most of all seasons. In all these changes we encounter defining moments—some that make us and some that break us.

Lessons are defined as something learned or taught. Listen to this story: A group of frogs were traveling through the woods, and two of the frogs fell into a very deep pit. All the other frogs gathered around the pit. When they saw how deep it was, they begin to yell to the other frogs. "Give up! Give up! It's too deep!

You will never get out." But the two frogs continued to leap. The frogs at the top of the pit continued to yell, "Give up and die." Well, one of the frogs listened to their comments and fell dead.

The other frogs that were gathered around the pit began to repeat the same comments. "Give up! Give up! You will never get out. Stop the pain and suffering and just die." The frog in the pit jumped even harder and finally, with all his might, the frog leaped out of the pit. Then the group of frogs gathered around and said to him, "Why didn't you listen to us, why didn't you give up?" The frog said, "I'm deaf and I thought you were encouraging me."

I learned two very important lessons from this frog:

    1.) Know when to turn a deaf ear.

    2.) Life and death are in the power of the tongue.

If someone is still in the pit, the pit of humiliation, the pit of aggravation, the pit of frustration, the pit of segregation, the pit of termination, the pit of isolation, the pit of discrimination, I stop by to say LEAP!

The End

P.S. God gave me double for my trouble and I won my case! Don't stop! You can get out of whatever pit life has thrown you into, Just leap!

Betty's Bits: A friend sent me this e-mail about the frog. However, I changed it according to my interpretation and I hope it blesses you the way it blessed me. The author is unknown. Just take a leap of faith!

You can't be a good solider

unless you are willing to

walk through

some mud! ENDURE

You must be willing to

make whatever

sacrifice necessary,

even if it means going through

the floods.

Where are the water walkers?

Betty Marie Knight

> ***Well, sacrifices***
> ***I had to make some,***
> ***as for***
> ***the water walkers,***
> ***it takes one to know one!***

Les Brown, motivational speaker, once said to me, "You need courage, faith and you have to be hun……..gry!" These words helped me to keep moving forward in my downtime. "Jump And Get Your Wings On the Way Down!"

    Thanks, Les
    Thanks, Shelley "Pepsi"

Silhouette Page

In our culture we were taught to watch what we say to people. In our Christian walk, we are taught to say things that are edifying

Corporate America: They Had A Plot But God Had A Plan
and comforting to the hearer. Remember the old cliché, "If you can't say anything nice don't say anything at all?"

Here are just a few things said to me by management and co-workers:

"Betty would you and ???? take your relationship outside?"

"Employees, do not speak to Betty or go to lunch with her."

"Betty get your butt up and leave now!"

"Betty the reason why we say these derogatory things to you are because we are jealous of you."

"Betty they can't hit a moving target so whatever you do Betty, bob and weave, bob and weave."

"Kick Betty's butt out of your office when she comes in here."

Employees communicated with me by walking pass my desk, whispering my name before throwing me a note. Negative comments undermines the confidence of the employee, yet I (Betty) was voted employee of the month!

Tell Me When And Where Did They Cross The Line?

Appendix A

This is how to file charges of discrimination at the Equal Employment Opportunity Commission (EEOC).

Causes of Discrimination:

☐ Race ☐ Color ☐ Sex ☐ Religion

☐ National Origin ☐ Retaliation ☐ Age

☐ Disability ☐ Other (specify)

Charge: Discrimination: In May of 1999, I was employed at ___ _____:

Charge: Harassment: In April 1999, co-workers and managers began to make derogatory slurs and offensive remarks daily to me _____.

Corporate America: They Had A Plot But God Had A Plan

Charge: Retaliation: In September 1998, after I informed the owner of the company of the harassment and the discrimination, retaliation immediately began on _____.

Charge: Sexual Advances: In June 2000, Mr. Peter said that _____.

Charge: Religious Harassment: On December 20, 2000 I have a right to pray and I also have a right not to pray in Corporate America._____.

Charge: Sex (gender) Racial Discrimination: On October 27, 2000, Sam Bing, a white male, and Jessie Ring, a black female, were reprimanded for the same service error. However, Jessie was written up and Sam was not.

Appendix B

Facts Sheets on Discrimination

Fact Sheets on Race/Color

Title VII of the Civil Rights Act of 1964 protects individuals against employment discrimination on the basis of race and color as well as national origin, sex, or religion.

It is unlawful to discriminate against any employee or applicant for employment because of his/her race or color in regard to hiring, termination, promotion, compensation, job training, or any other term, condition, or privilege of employment. Title VII also prohibits employment decisions based on stereotypes and assumptions about abilities, traits, or the performances of individuals of certain racial groups. Title VII prohibits both intentional discrimination and neutral job policies that disproportionately exclude minorities and that are not job related.

Equal employment opportunity cannot be denied because of marriage to or association with an individual of a different race; membership in or association with ethnic based organizations or groups; or attendance or participation in schools or places of worship generally associated with minority groups.

Race-Related Characteristics and Conditions

Discrimination on the basis of an immutable characteristic associated with race, such as skin color, hair texture, or certain facial features violates Title VII, even though not all members of the race share the same characteristics.

Title VII also prohibits discrimination on the basis of a condition, which predominantly affects one race unless the practice is job related and consistent with business necessity. For example, since sickle cell anemia predominantly occurs in African-Americans, a policy, which excludes individuals with sickle cell anemia, must be job related and consistent with business necessity. Similarly, a "no-beard" employment policy may discriminate against African-

American men who have a predisposition to pseudofolliculitis barbae (severe shaving bumps) unless the policy is job related and consistent with business necessity.

Harassment

Harassment on the basis of race and/or color violates Title VII. Ethnic slurs, racial "jokes," offensive or derogatory comments, or other verbal or physical conduct based on an individual's race/color constitutes unlawful harassment if the conduct creates an intimidating, hostile, or offensive working environment, or interferes with the individual's work performance.

Facts About Sexual Harassment

Sexual harassment is a form of sex discrimination that violates Title VII of the Civil Rights Act 1964.

Unwelcome sexual advances, request for sexual favors and verbal physical conduct of a sexual nature constitute sexual harassment when submission to our rejection of this conduct explicitly or implicitly affects an individual's employment, unreasonably interferes with an individual's work performance or creates an intimidating, hostile, or offensive work environment.

Sexual harassment can occur in a variety of circumstances, including but not limited to the following:

The victim as well as the harasser may be a woman or a man. The victim does not have to be of the opposite sex. The harasser can be the victim's supervisor, agent of the employer, a supervisor in another area, a co-worker, or a non-employee. The victim does not have to be the person harassed but could be anyone affected by the offensive conduct. (Third-Party Harassment) Unlawful sexual harassment may occur without economic injury to or discharge of the victim.

The harasser's conduct must be unwelcome. It is helpful for the victim to directly inform the harasser that the conduct is unwelcome and must stop. The victim should use any employer complaint mechanism or grievance system available.

When investigating allegations of sexual harassment, EEOC looks at the whole record: the circumstances, such as the nature of the sexual advances, and the context in which the alleged incidents occurred. A determination on the allegations is made from the facts on a case-by-case basis.

Prevention is the best tool to eliminate sexual harassment in the workplace. Employers are encouraged to takes steps necessary to prevent sexual harassment from occurring. They should clearly communicate to employees that sexual harassment will not be tolerated. They can do so by establishing an effective complaint or grievance process and taking immediate and appropriate action when an employee complains.

Facts About Religion

Title VII of the Civil Rights Act of 1964 prohibits employers from discriminating against individuals because of their religion in hiring, firing, and other terms and conditions of employment. The Act also requires employers to reasonably accommodate the religious practices of an employee or prospective employee, unless to do so would create an undue hardship upon the employer. Flexible scheduling, voluntary substitutions or swaps, job reassignments and lateral transfers are examples of accommodating an employee's religious beliefs.

Facts About Pregnancy

The Pregnancy Discrimination Act is and amendment to Title VII of the Civil Rights Act of 1964. Discrimination on the basis of pregnancy, childbirth or related medical conditions constitutes unlawful sex discrimination under Title VII. Women affected by pregnancy or related conditions must be treated in the same manner as other applicants or employees with similar abilities or limitations.

Hiring

An employer cannot refuse to hire a woman because of her pregnancy related condition as long as she is able to perform the major functions of the job. An employer cannot refuse to hire her because of its prejudices against pregnant workers or the prejudices of co-workers, client or customers, etc.

Facts About The Americans with Disabilities Act

Title I of the Americans with Disabilities Act 1990, which takes effect July 26, 1992, prohibits private employers, state and local governments, employment agencies and labor unions from discriminating against qualified individuals with disabilities in job application procedures, hiring firing, advancement, compensation, job training, and other terms, conditions and privileges of employment. An individual with a disability is a person who has a physical or mental impairment that substantially limits one or more major life activities; has a record of such an impairment; or is regarded as having such on impairment.

A qualified individual with a disability is an individual who, with or without reasonable accommodation, can perform the essential functions of the job in question.

Facts about Color Discrimination

Pre-Employment Inquiries - Requesting pre-employment information, which discloses or tends to disclose an applicant's race suggests that the race will be unlawfully used as a basis for hiring. Solicitation of such pre-employment information is presumed to be used as a basis for making selection decisions. Therefore, if members of minority groups are excluded from employment, the request for such pre-employment information would likely constitute evidence of discrimination.

Segregation and Classification of Employees

Title VII is violated where minority employees are segregated by physically isolating them from other employees from customer contact. Title VII also prohibits assigning primarily minorities to predominantly minority establishments or geographic areas. It is also illegal to exclude minorities from certain positions or to group or categorize employees or jobs so that minorities generally hold certain jobs. Coding applications/resumes to designate an

Corporate America: They Had A Plot But God Had A Plan

applicant's race, by either an employer or employment or from certain positions.

Betty's Bits: Please stop by your EEOC office and pick up fact sheets on all the different discriminations that violate our Civil and Constitutional Rights. Department of Fair Employment Housing is another office to file a charge of discrimination with—this office seems to obtain a quicker resolve. The Labor Board is another avenue an employee can travel. The EEOC took about two years to handle my charge; the Department of Fair Employment and Housing handled several friends of mine within 6-8 months. These procedures can vary in different states. In the state of California the process seem to be a little slower.

Attention

This ten-year experience has qualified me to speak at presentations, seminars, conferences, and workshops concerning Corporate America.

If you are interested in my addressing these matters on a more personal note, please contact me at:

Betty M. Knight

Hawthorne, California 90250

(310) ____-_____

www. ----- ------ ----.com

BIBLIOGRAPHY

Title VII of the Civil Rights Act of 1964

The U.S. Equal Employment Opportunity Commission

Title VII of the Civil Rights Act of 1964 protects individuals against employment discrimination on the basis of race and color as well as national origin, sex, or religion.

Address: 255 East Temple Street, Los Angeles, Ca. 90012

Federal Laws Prohibiting Job Discrimination Questions and Answers: The Civil Rights Act of 1991, which, among others things, provides monetary damages in cases of intentional employment discrimination.

Fact Sheets are available in alternative formats, upon request.

Betty Marie Knight

    Facts About Race/Color Discrimination

    Facts About Sex Discrimination

    Facts About Sexual Discrimination

    Facts About National Origin Discrimination

    Facts About Religion Discrimination

    Facts About Harassment Discrimination

    Facts About Retaliation Discrimination

Web-site: http://www.opm.gov/er/address 2/guide01.htm; OSC at (202) 653-7188

Spielberg, S. (Director) (1997) Schindler's list [Videotape]. Los Angeles: Viacom. "Armistad."

Tillman, G. (Director) (2000) Schindler's list [Videotape]. Los Angeles: Viacom." Men of Honor"

Johnson, C. (Director) (2001) Schindler's list [Videotape]. Los Angeles: Viacom. "Boycott"

Apted, M. (Director) (2002) Schindler's list [Videotape]. Los Angeles: Viacom. "Enough"

Thompson, G (Director) (2000) Schindler's list [Videotape]. Los Angeles: Viacom. "Hollow Man"

Corporate America: They Had A Plot But God Had A Plan

Books

Within the Plantation Household: Black and White Women of the Old South: Fox-Genovese, Elizabeth, and 1941-The University, of North Carolina Press.

Dear America, when Christmas comes again: the World War I diary Simone Spencer by Levine, Beth Seidel. C2002 Scholastic Inc.

Dictionary

Black's Law Dictionary with pronunciations. 6th edition Blacks, Henry Campbell-by the publishers' editorial staff; contributing author, Joseph R. Nolan...{Ed al.}

Webster's New World Dictionary Prentice-Hall Student Edition

The America Heritage Children's Dictionary Copyright 1998 by Houghton Mifflin Company.

Webster's Crossword Puzzle Dictionary 1997 PSL Association Inc. Copyright MCMIXIV Fawcett Publisher Inc printed in the USA

E-Mail, "A Lesson from a Frog" author unknown

Poem, 23rd Psalm in the Workplace author unknown

Betty Marie Knight

E-Mail, "Being Black In The Work Place of America," author unknown

(www.infonet.com, page 143 the chapter on Communication)

Spiros, Zodhiates. Zohiates' The Hebrew Greek Key Study Bible 1984 and 1991, AMG International References DBA/ AMG Publishers. Tyndale House Publishers, Inc., Wheaton, Il. 60189. All rights reserved. Copyright 1988, 1989, 1990, 1991, 1993, 1996. The bible text used in this edition of the Life Application Study Bibles is the Holy Bible King James Version.

KJV Standard Lesson Commentary 2003-2004 edited by Ronald G. Davis, Ronald L. Nickelson, and Jonathan Underwood, International Sunday School Lessons.

Maxwell, John C., 1947- The 21 Irrefutable laws of Leadership: Follow them and People Will Follow You/ John C. Maxwell

Monroe, Myle., The Purpose and Power of God's Glory

Webster Dictionary: R. F. PATTERSON, M.A., D. Litt. 1988 Edition Published by PSI & Associates, Inc. Miami, Florida

Crowd, S. "What Do You Do When Strangling is not an Option?" article

Corporate America: They Had A Plot But God Had A Plan
Speakers: Other Sources

Chironna, M.

Dunphy, J.

Jakes, T.D.

Jones, N.

Monroe, M.

Picture

Friend of the family 9-1-1

About the Author

Betty Marie Knight was born on January 6, in a small town called Jonesboro, Arkansas. Betty attended Booker T. Washington in Jonesboro, Arkansas. One year prior to desegregation at Booker T. Washington. Betty faced integration at Hillcrest Elementary, a white school in which Betty feels prepared her for what she endured throughout Corporate America. Even as a young child enduring integration in the South Betty demonstrated her leadership skills by being one of first children to endure the birth pains of desegregation. In 1972 Betty began academic studies at Arkansas State University in Elementary Education. Betty traveled to Aschaffenburg, Germany where she studied European Culture for three years. In 1978, Betty returned to the United States and began her pursuit for God in a greater way. In

1987, God spoke to Betty and said, "Speak my Word and I will move for you." Betty has been speaking the WORD of God ever since. In 1981, Betty M. Knight began service in the prophetic ministry of Pastor Arturo Spates and Patricia Spates. In 1983, Betty Knight finished her curriculums at Los Angeles Southwest College where she received an Associate Arts Degree in Theater Arts, and Business where Betty went ahead and obtained a Real Estate Sales License for the State of California. On the completion of her studies at Southwest College, Betty Knight is currently pursing a career in Special Education. Betty Knight is also a licensed minister at the City Of Refuge under the leadership of Bishop Noel Jones.

Printed in the United States
25300LVS00004B/94-105